More Praise for *Awakening Compassion*

"Work is a place where most of us spend a large percentage ui uu. ...
Yet for many, the workplace remains a source of stress and anxiety. In their land-
mark book, Worline and Dutton give us an overview of the problem and science-
based solutions. It will help individuals not only in the workplace but in their
lives. For the employer, it is a powerful tool to give employees meaning in their
work and to increase creativity, productivity, and ultimately shareholder value."

—**James R. Doty, MD, Clinical Professor of Neurosurgery and founder and
Director of the Center for Compassion and Altruism Research and Education,
Stanford University School of Medicine, and *New York Times* bestselling author
of *Into the Magic Shop***

"*The* go-to book on the hottest new trend in the corporate world: compassion.
Worline and Dutton have spent years researching *positive deviance*: how to
bring greater humanity to the workplace. Their work is groundbreaking: a compassionate workplace is happier, healthier, and more productive. Packed with
real-world examples of the many companies they have advised and researched,
Awakening Compassion at Work is for all those who want to see themselves
and their company succeed to its full potential."

—**Emma Seppälä, PhD, Science Director, Center for Compassion and Altruism
Research and Education, Stanford University, and author of *The Happiness Track***

"In today's ever so fast-paced, technological, and profit-driven world, our humanity in the workplace is all too often passed over or even forgotten. *Awakening
Compassion at Work* not only contains memorable examples of noticing, interpreting, feeling, and acting on suffering in the workplace but also provides a tool
kit for engaging colleagues in using compassionate actions to create new norms
and routines that nurture our bonding together and resilience to innovate, collaborate, and improve our work environment. I highly recommend that you read
this enjoyable and forward-thinking book to awaken your compassionate self,
not only at work, but also at home."

—**Roger Newton, Executive Chairman and Chief Scientific Officer, Esperion
Therapeutics, Inc.**

"Seldom do we get a gift that helps us step outside of our self-centered lives into
noticing and caring about others—beyond feeling for them to helping reduce suffering and make others' lives and work fulfilling. Worline and Dutton offer us the
emotional glue that binds our social fabric in organizations and cultures through
compassion. Steeped in rigorous research but without the obfuscation of aca-
demia, the book draws you in with engaging stories and gives you hope with the
authors' exercises and guidance in how to reduce the toxicity of guilt and blame
and create a new social architecture of caring. Read it—it will fill your soul!"

—**Richard Boyatzis, PhD, Distinguished University Professor, Departments of
Psychology, Cognitive Science, and Organizational Behavior, Case Western**

"Monica Worline and Jane Dutton are the world's experts on the subject of compassion in organizations. Theirs was the first research conducted on this topic almost two decades ago, and their insight and practical wisdom is captured in this volume. This is *the* statement on what we know and what we can do about the subject of compassion in organizations."

—Kim Cameron, PhD, William Russell Kelly Professor of Management and Organizations, Ross School of Business, and Professor of Higher Education, School of Education, University of Michigan

"With *Awakening Compassion at Work*, Monica Worline and Jane Dutton bring to bear their academic brilliance, sizable hands-on experience in business and psychology, and a gift for getting to the core of a principle that is essential to individual and organizational success. Using in-depth research, collaborative explorations in first-rate organizations, a boatload of meaningful and moving examples, and practical guidelines for igniting the remarkable power of compassion, the authors have fashioned an essential, pragmatic, and fascinating book that will be riveting reading for anyone in the workplace."

—Ari Cowan, Director General, The International Center for Compassionate Organizations

"In our rapid-change, hypercompetitive, and global economy, encountering a compassionate leader can be rare; being embraced within a compassionate organization culture even more so. In contrast to this harsh organizational anthropology, Worline and Dutton set forth with conceptual clarity and rich exemplification practices that empirically lead toward a compassionate organizational milieu. Any leader perusing this manuscript will experience a shift in consciousness. Enacting the new wisdom will radically change an organization's culture."

—André L. Delbecq, PhD, Professor of Management and Senior Fellow, Ignatian Center for Jesuit Education, Santa Clara University

"If you are one of the many who think compassion has no place in business, read this book. Extraordinary performance comes from tapping into the full power of your team. After more than thirty years in business, one thing is clear to me: compassion is central in a culture that gets extraordinary results."

—David Drews, founder and CEO, Justus Equity, LLC

"Suffering is inevitable and can reveal itself anytime, anywhere. This inspiring book will transport you into work worlds that dare to care. Discoveries from the Compassion Lab spring to life in vivid stories of how compassion and work go hand in hand in successful organizations. Most importantly, Worline and Dutton offer practical guidance on how to reshape the social architecture of your organizations to support the improvisation of authentic compassionate acts. This book holds the power to open hearts worldwide."

—**Barbara L. Fredrickson, PhD, Kenan Distinguished Professor of Psychology and Neuroscience, The University of North Carolina at Chapel Hill, and author of *Positivity* and *Love 2.0***

"Groundbreaking! Based on fifteen years of scholarly research, this book makes the case for compassion in the workplace—both interpersonally and systemically—and offers a clear blueprint for how to do it. The authors offer design principles and nuanced examples that reflect the day-to-day reality of organizational life, encouraging and empowering readers to go out and try it for themselves. This book is destined to change many lives for the better."

—**Christopher Germer, PhD, faculty, Harvard Medical School, author of *The Mindful Path to Self-Compassion*, and co-editor of *Mindfulness and Psychotherapy***

"What we produce and how we produce the goods and services all around us is one of the most important human issues of our age. From the sweatshops of Asia to the boardrooms of high technology, we know that there can be considerable competitive pressures that cause great stress and at times deeply immoral behavior. Dutton and Worline are world leaders and pioneers in the extraordinarily important turn toward more compassionate work. Here is a book that outlines in detail some of the challenges a compassionate approach to work confronts and how to deal with them. This is an outstanding book that will be a classic for years to come. It will aid greatly the human endeavor to create a more compassionate world."

—**Paul Gilbert, PhD, FBPsS, OBE, Professor, Centre for Compassion Research and Training, College of Health and Social Care Research Centre, University of Derby**

"Hurrah! Worline and Dutton have made the business case for compassion and created a road map for bringing it to life in any organization. Their courage and clear seeing lead us to a more productive and positive future."

—**Edi Pasalis, MBA, MTS, Director, Kripalu Institute for Extraordinary Living**

"Workplaces are often toxic and actually give rise to human suffering. Drawing on extensive research, the authors show the many positive outcomes of recognizing and confronting this truth. With great skill they show us how to create organizations that alleviate suffering and awaken compassion. This is a must-read that will be with us for a very long time."

—Robert E. Quinn, PhD, Professor, Ross School of Business, University of Michigan, and author of *The Positive Organization*

"The value of this book is that it clearly articulates not only why but how to stimulate cultural elements that will make alleviation of suffering through compassion an everyday occurrence for any organization that desires to do so. I am blown away with the authors' ability to move this complex and oft-avoided concept of compassion into an easily accessible initiative for any organization. Not only does this benefit individuals experiencing suffering, but thanks to the clear strategies for implementation, profound cultural strengthening can occur."

—Fred Keller, founder and Chair, Cascade Engineering

AWAKENING COMPASSION
at WORK

AWAKENING
COMPASSION
at WORK

The Quiet Power
That Elevates People
and Organizations

Monica C. Worline

Jane E. Dutton

BK

Berrett–Koehler Publishers, Inc.
a BK Business book

BERRETT-KOEHLER PUBLISHERS, INC.
1333 Broadway, Suite 1000, Oakland, CA 94612-1921
Tel: (510) 817-2277   Fax: (510) 817-2278   www.bkconnection.com

Ordering Information

Quantity Sales. Special discounts are available on quantity purchases by corporations, associations, and others. For details, contact the "Special Sales Department" at the Berrett-Koehler address above.

Individual Sales. Berrett-Koehler publications are available through most bookstores. They can also be ordered directly from Berrett-Koehler: Tel: (800) 929-2929; Fax: (802) 864-7626; www.bkconnection.com

Orders for College Textbook/Course Adoption Use. Please contact Berrett-Koehler: Tel: (800) 929-2929; Fax: (802) 864-7626.

Orders by U.S. Trade Bookstores and Wholesalers. Please contact Ingram Publisher Services, Tel: (800) 509-4887; Fax: (800) 838-1149; E-mail: customer.service@ ingrampublisherservices.com; or visit www.ingrampublisherservices.com/Ordering for details about electronic ordering.

Berrett-Koehler and the BK logo are registered trademarks of Berrett-Koehler Publishers, Inc.

Printed in Canada

Berrett-Koehler books are printed on long-lasting acid-free paper. When it is available, we choose paper that has been manufactured by environmentally responsible processes. These may include using trees grown in sustainable forests, incorporating recycled paper, minimizing chlorine in bleaching, or recycling the energy produced at the paper mill.

Library of Congress Cataloging-in-Publication Data

Names: Worline, Monica C., author. | Dutton, Jane E., author.
Title: Awakening compassion at work : the quiet power that elevates people and organizations / Monica C. Worline, Ph.D., Jane E. Dutton, Ph.D.
Description: Oakland, CA : Berrett-Koehler Publishers, [2017] | Includes bibliographical references.
Identifiers: LCCN 2016038078 | ISBN 9781626564459 (pbk.)
Subjects: LCSH: Organizational behavior. | Compassion. | Management--Psychological aspects.
Classification: LCC HD58.7 .W676 2017 | DDC 658.3/12--dc23
LC record available at https://lccn.loc.gov/2016038078

First Edition

22 21 20 19 18 17   10 9 8 7 6 5 4 3 2 1

Interior design: Laura Lind Design
Cover/jacket design: Leslie Waltzer/Crowfoot Design
Production service: Linda Jupiter Productions
Edit: Elissa Rabellino
Proofread: Karen Hill Green
Index: Paula C. Durbin-Westby

For Peter Frost, who was with us in every word.

CONTENTS

FOREWORD

A FEW YEARS AGO, I came across a billboard on a New York City bus shelter. It read, "If your company cared, it would be in the caring business." The ad was for a jobs site, and the message was clear: the vast majority of companies do not care, and the best thing you can do is to find another company that also doesn't care, but where you may be somewhat better off.

This cynical but sadly true message is symptomatic of the dominant business culture that exists in the world today. The old clichés about business all still ring true: it is a dog-eat-dog world out there, nice guys finish last, only the paranoid survive, and, most tellingly, "It's not personal, it's business." Business has become dehumanized and impersonal. Human beings are treated as functions or objects, as interchangeable and disposable as machine parts. No wonder employee engagement levels are shockingly low, according to Gallup: less than 30 percent in the United States and only about 13 percent worldwide. The vast majority of people are dispirited and uninspired at work. They feel disrespected, not listened to, and devalued.

Human beings have extraordinary, almost divine capacities. Yet the vast majority of people never get to realize that potential because they are embedded in organizational systems that fail to promote human flourishing. As the expression goes, most people die with their music still inside them. To bring about flourishing, we must pay attention to the "seed" as well as the "soil"—the people as well as the organizational context. Even the most extraordinary seed cannot thrive in toxic soil. Ordinary human beings today are in fact extraordinary, by any historical measure. For one thing, we are astonishingly more intelligent; as unearthed in the Flynn effect, a person whose IQ is considered average today would have tested in the top 2 percent of IQ a mere 80 years ago. What we have today are millions of extraordinary beings stuck in debilitatingly dysfunctional organizations.

The symptoms of this are everywhere. "Thank God it's Friday" is a sentiment that most working people can readily identify with, so much so that it inspired the name of a popular restaurant chain. People dread going to work and eagerly look forward to their time outside of work—often using drugs and alcohol to dull their pain. We have the sad and stark reality that heart attacks are the highest on Monday mornings, by at least 20 percent compared with other days. More than wars, murderers, and terrorists, our work is literally killing us. As Fred Kofman wrote in *Conscious Business*, "There are no death camps in corporations, but many apparently successful companies hide great suffering in their basements."

How can we change this sad reality? We must pay urgent attention to the qualities of the workplaces that we are creating. We must create environments in which people are inspired, feel safe, are cared for, and receive recognition and celebration for who they are and what they do. More than anything else, this requires that we create truly human workplaces that are instilled with a deep sense of compassion, the subject of this important book.

We live in a world of extraordinary pain and suffering. While conditions today are less vicious and brutal than they have been for much of human history, the reality remains that billions of people face a daily struggle for survival and dignity. In such a world, it is imperative that, individually as well as through our organizations, we work toward alleviating the suffering and bringing greater joy. Therefore, every organizational and personal purpose at some level needs to be a healing purpose. If we are not part of the healing, we are part of the hurting. Healing begins with compassion. That is the master key.

Compassion is rooted in a fundamental human drive: the need to care. Human beings have at least three primary drives: self-interest, the need to care, and, increasingly, the need to live a life of meaning and purpose. Unfortunately, we built our system of capitalism on the pillar of self-interest alone. Our need to care is at least as strong as, if not stronger than, our drive toward self-interest. But we have created a world of work in which we are asked to check our humanity at the door, in which there is little to no room for caring. The most human aspects of what it means to be a human being have thus been left out of work. This is an extraordinary deficit for which we have collectively paid a steep price. As Jane Dutton has written previously, organizations can suppress or amplify the human capacity for caring. Unfortunately, most organizations have become hostile to this most human of drives.

Extraordinary things happen when caring and compassion are expressed in the context of work. In 1980, when Whole Foods Market was very early in its journey, with only one store in Austin, Texas, the city experienced one of the worst floods in its history. Many people were killed, and the damage was extensive, including to the Whole Foods store, which was essentially decimated. All the equipment and inventory were destroyed. The company had no warehoused inventory, no more credit, and no financial resources to fall back on. Nearly half a million dollars in the red on that day, the company was essentially bankrupt. What rescued the business and set it on its path to becoming a $14 billion company that has had a huge impact on the food business and on the lives of countless millions? It was the caring and compassion shown by its stakeholders on that fateful day. Customers and neighbors showed up at the store to help clean up the mess, working shoulder to shoulder with employees for weeks to get the store back in shape. Employees worked without any guarantee that they would get paid, since the company's leaders had no idea how they could restart. Seeing the extraordinary outpouring of support, many of the company suppliers offered to absorb much of the losses and restock the store on credit. Bankers decided to extend more credit to the company, even though there was no logical justification for doing so. The original investors in the business decided to reinvest additional money into the enterprise. Impromptu groups sprang up to organize concerts and other community events to raise money—for a business! Within weeks, the store was able to reopen, and the company was on its way to eventually becoming a transformational force in the culture.

There is no greater power or source of strength in the world than love. As His Holiness the Dalai Lama has said, "Love and compassion are necessities, not luxuries. Without them, humanity cannot survive." Yet the vast majority of companies continue to shy away from elevating love, caring, and compassion in the workplace. I believe this has a lot to do with the reality that the vast majority of businesses continue to be run by men, based on a very limited set of hypermasculine values, such as domination, aggression, ambition, competition, winning at all costs, short-term thinking, and a zero-sum view of the world. We're fortunate to be living in a time when feminine qualities such as relationships, nurturing, compassion, vulnerability, caring, and cooperation are finally being recognized, not as signs of weakness but as sources of great strength. These are the most human of qualities that have been sidelined for just about all of human history. It is high time that they were brought to the fore, and we're fortunate to be living at a time when that seems attainable.

Written by two extraordinary women, this book embodies this wisdom. *Awakening Compassion at Work* is a timely and critically important book. It powerfully makes the humanistic as well as business case for greater compassion in the workplace, and then provides clear guidance for how to make that happen. Written by two of the foremost scholars in the subject, the book reflects their extensive practical experience helping companies awaken to and then implement these ideas. I am grateful to Monica and Jane for their life's work, which has culminated in this outstanding book.

Raj Sisodia
F. W. Olin Distinguished Professor of Global Business,
Babson College Co-founder and Co-chairman, Conscious Capitalism Inc.

PART ONE

AN INTRODUCTION TO SUFFERING, COMPASSION, AND WORK

Suffering is a heavy word. Most of the time, we try to avoid it. *Suffering* is also a word you might not connect to work life. Suffering doesn't typically show up on lists of businesses' most significant concerns or make the cut of the many issues that can occupy a manager's agenda. But it should. A new science of compassion, based in extensive research, helps us to see that suffering, and the compassion that helps address suffering directly, is one of the most important ideas for business today.

Most of us will spend at least one hundred thousand hours of our lives at work. Some of us will spend a lot more. It's either foolish or wishful thinking to imagine that suffering—a concept fundamental to human existence—could be separate from this immense investment of time and energy. But even if we know that people suffer, should businesses or work organizations care? Isn't the suffering of life separate from the demands of work? We might believe those statements, but our and others' research has shown that suffering at work is a hidden cost to human capability.[1] Recognizing this costly oversight, smart employees, managers, and leaders who care deeply about the capacity of their organizations to operate with full human effectiveness will pay more attention to awakening compassion at work.

WHAT IS COMPASSION AT WORK?

SUFFERING NEVER REALLY CROSSED ANDY'S mind, especially not as a hidden cost to his organization. But one day as he was running a meeting, a standout employee on his engineering team was unusually quiet and distant. Not knowing how to interpret this, Andy stood next to Xian as he was getting coffee during a break. He asked if everything was OK. Shocking Andy with the intensity of his grief, Xian told him that his sister, who lived in China and had planned to come to the United States to study, had been killed in a tragic accident. Feeling that there was nothing he could do at home, and drawn to be with his colleagues, Xian had chosen to come to work. Xian told Andy that sinking into the technical details of the meeting provided a kind of relief from the tide of memories that otherwise washed over him.

Facing this news, Andy needed to make a choice as a manager— one that his MBA curriculum and leadership development training hadn't prepared him to make. Was he going to regard Xian's life outside of work as a valid and important part of the ongoing situation he was managing, or was he going to treat Xian's life, and the loss of his sister, as if they were outside work bounds?

Death has a way of making these considerations starker. Andy invited Xian to take time off if he needed it, to talk with him at any time, and even to come to Andy's own home and spend time with his family. Not all managers would have made the same decision. The depth and quality of relationships at work are part of the complex landscape of suffering and compassion that we will explore together in this book. Andy's choice to pay attention to Xian's grief, to understand it as relevant to the work of managing, to connect with empathy and concern, and to act on those feelings offers a lived example that is like thousands of other examples we have gathered and analyzed in our research over the past fifteen years.[1] What may seem like small interpersonal moves on Andy's part were actually potent for alleviating suffering.

But what if Xian had not been a star performer? What if the loss of his sister hadn't seemed so obviously relevant? What if the grief had diminished Xian's capacity to contribute to the team? Would Andy's calculus as a manager have been different? What if Xian had mentioned to Andy on the coffee break that his sister had suffered from a mental breakdown? Or that she had a gambling addiction and had thrown the family into bankruptcy? The forms that suffering takes matter for compassion. How suffering resonates with cultural and organizational values is also part of the complex landscape of compassion at work. We don't aim to provide easy answers, but we do draw on two decades of work in this field to deepen your capacity to think about complicated human dilemmas and how to handle them.

Most managers like Andy worry—separate from their personal feelings of empathy and concern toward their employees—about critical questions related to compassion in the workplace. Will employees who are treated with compassion take advantage of their managers or their organizations? Will compassion toward one member of the team, like Xian, set a precedent that locks the manager or organization into a costly pattern of action in the future? Will Andy be able to be fair to others if he opens his heart to Xian's suffering? Will he look weak to the leaders who evaluate him if he offers flexibility to his staff? Addressing and overcoming these concerns is a fundamental aim of this book.

WHAT IS COMPASSION?

As organizational scholars, we study compassion from a social scientific point of view. Compassion is more than an emotion; it is a felt and enacted desire to alleviate suffering. We define it as a four-part process that involves: (1) noticing that suffering is present in an organization, (2) making meaning of suffering in a way that contributes to a desire to alleviate it, (3) feeling empathic concern for the people suffering, and (4) taking action to alleviate suffering in some manner.[2] This definition highlights the fact that compassion is a multipart process. We will explore in Part Two: Awakening Compassion in Our Work Lives how each aspect is affected by both human and organizational factors.

It's also notable that compassion always unfolds in relation to suffering. This differentiates compassion from other positive interpersonal concepts such as kindness, gratitude, and happiness. Kindness, for example, is a desire to voluntarily and proactively support another person's flourishing, while happiness is a personal sense of well-being. Gratitude involves feeling and expressing appreciation for a life experience. Experiences of happiness, gratitude, and kindness are important to developing a positive side of work.

They are central concepts in the study of positive psychology, and research supports their role in cultivating mental, emotional, and physical health.[3] Compassion contrasts with these in that it is explicitly linked to the shadow or darker side of life; compassion goes hand-in-hand with suffering. But it isn't all dark. Because it deeply bonds us with others, compassion is wired into our brains and bodies in ways that motivate and reward us for responding to suffering.[4] Compassion is central to human well-being, for those who provide it as well as for those who receive it. But because it encompasses both negative and positive, the dark and light sides of life, it isn't always simple.

COMPASSION IN ORGANIZATIONS

Organizations matter in two ways when we want to understand compassion at work. First, workplaces provide a context that shapes what we notice, think, feel, and do as individuals. Second, workplaces are filled with people and resources that can be coordinated more or less competently to alleviate suffering. We look closely at both the individual and the organizational levels in this book.

One way to understand the powerful role of organizations in awakening compassion is to engage in a thought experiment about a specific instance of suffering, such as when members lose their homes in a fire. We have studied responses to the same kind of loss in different organizations and found very different patterns of compassion. Imagine one workplace where the organization is widely known as a great place to work, and members come to the organization with explicit values of taking care of one another. These values help position a loss of a home in a fire as relevant to the work community. Because it is important to care for people at work in this organization, it's easier for people to feel empathy for the loss and step in to begin organizing action to alleviate the impact of the fire. It is seen as an appropriate and legitimate use of time and of the organization's formal communication methods to organize action.

In another organization, an announcement about a fire that destroyed employees' homes lands in a busy, high-pressure workplace where competition is rampant. People who open the announcement in their crowded email boxes feel a fleeting sense of concern, but this concern has to compete with budget concerns that receive more discussion. Many people don't pay much attention to the announcement at all. They are focused on trying to one-up each other and keep their positions in the next round of layoffs. While the people who do hear of the loss wish there was something they could do, they don't view it as legitimate to use the organization's formal channels to organize about nontask issues, so they end up doing nothing. There's no easy way to turn their concern into action, so feelings of empathy melt away under the pressures of the next deadline.

Notice that the two organizations in our thought experiment are each composed of kind people. But despite this fact, compassion unfolds very differently. In Part Three: Awakening Compassion Competence in Organizations, we will show in greater depth how elements of an organization such as network ties between people, cultural values, work roles, routines, and actions of leaders matter in creating these patterns of compassion that vary across organizations. While cultivating compassion in the individual members of organizations is helpful and important to awakening compassion, it is not enough. Understanding how structures and processes in organizations make it easier or harder to express compassion—not just at the interpersonal level but also at the systemic level—is essential for awakening compassion at work. It is this system-level organizational focus that is the distinctive emphasis of our research and this book.

KEY POINTS: DEFINING COMPASSION AT WORK

∞ Compassion is a felt and enacted desire to alleviate suffering.

∞ Compassion is defined as a four-part process involving attention, interpretation of suffering, felt empathic concern, and action to alleviate suffering.

∞ Suffering is pervasive in workplaces.

∞ Common sources of suffering flow from outside work boundaries, when people suffer from illness, injury, loss, divorce, financial pressures, addiction, or other hardships.

∞ Forms of suffering arise from work itself, through downsizing, restructuring, change processes, the stress of heavy workloads, performance pressure, feeling devalued, disrespectful interactions, and other organizational sources.

BREAKING THE SILENCE ABOUT SUFFERING AT WORK

When we recently asked members of one organization where we were doing research to name sources of suffering, they spoke of a lack of appreciation for their talents and skills, of being at the whim of supervisors who didn't understand the difficulties of their work, of pressure of unreasonable deadlines and demands, and of feeling consistently devalued and disengaged when they wanted their work to be meaningful. These are pervasive forms of suffering at work. So pervasive, in fact, that they likely are taken for granted as part of the work environment and slip under the surface of everyday work life.

Of course there are many sources of suffering outside of work as well. Employees like Xian remind us of the suffering that flows from deaths or illnesses in families and life losses such as divorces and separations. Suffering arises from stresses in family roles, financial difficulties, addictions, and many more hardships. While these forms of suffering don't originate within workplaces, they nonetheless seep in from outside. Silent suffering colors work.[5]

An additional source of suffering comes from organizations themselves, often through policies such as restructuring or downsizing, or as a result of change efforts and heavy workloads. It's easy to overlook or dismiss this suffering. Managers and leaders may assume it's not important or it will go away on its own without their attention. But organizations that create pain can also address it with compassion. In fact, our work shows that the very best organizations, leaders, and managers regard this as a fundamental part of their work.[6]

Research shows that compassion for this kind of pain leads to more adaptability and more effective change processes, which are part of the strategic significance of compassion at work that we will discuss in chapter 2. There are other benefits as well. Patty's story, which is adapted from our research, illustrates how an organization can create suffering during change. It also reveals a few ways that compassion at work would enhance both Patty's well-being and the effectiveness of the organization. Patty loved her work as an executive assistant assigned to several leaders. She found joy in building close relationships with them and used her personal knowledge about their likes and dislikes to anticipate their needs. Patty was masterful at recruiting resources that were maximally helpful, even before being asked. Executives she supported sometimes joked that Patty could read their minds. So when Patty received an email late one Friday afternoon telling her that she was being moved to a shared services group, she was surprised. The message told her that all executive and administrative assistants would now take work from a central pool. She felt shocked and devastated. None of the executives she supported were in the office this late on a Friday, so she had no one to ask about the change. Without anyone to help her make sense of the message, Patty spent the weekend worried and trying to understand what it meant for her.

First thing Monday morning, Patty arrived at her usual cubicle to find a moving trolley and boxes. She was instructed to pack as quickly as possible. She had to change locations before she'd had a chance to interact with anyone. The rush left her no time to say good-bye. The fact that she moved to a distant building made it hard for people she'd worked closely with in the past to find her. Patty began to do work from the request pool. While she was still an efficient employee, her daily experience of work changed dramatically. Online requests had to be fulfilled without knowing the people or the story behind them. Patty's magic talent of "mind reading" disappeared with this lack of relational connection. The change diminished Patty's sense of her own competence and creativity. She still received warm smiles and an occasional comment like "We miss you!" from the leaders she had worked with before. But given the new structure, Patty now found herself lonely, isolated, and often bored by work that had previously been a source of joy and inspiration.

In Patty's case, an efficiency-oriented change created suffering as a by-product. Those who design and implement efficiency-oriented changes like these often give little consideration to how the process could be done in ways that minimize suffering. Managers and leaders likewise give little consideration to how they could alleviate suffering in the aftermath of change. But this book will show you that, while suffering might be inevitable, there are many opportunities for awakening compassion at work.

Let's consider Patty's case. How could her organization have implemented change with greater compassion competence? Five steps would have increased compassion without decreasing efficiency. First, the timing of the communication could have been adjusted with attention to suffering, so that Patty did not have to make sense of the change alone over a weekend. Second, those implementing the change could have explicitly linked it with the overall culture and values of the organization that gave worth and dignity to support staff, making the change more meaningful to Patty and elevating her role rather than diminishing it. Third, the organization could have adjusted the relocation routines so that people who cared about Patty knew how to find her and the sense of disconnection was minimized. Fourth, the organization could host a celebration in the service of embracing change, formally recognizing those who were moving into the support pool and also creating a chance to say a festive good-bye. And finally, the manager in the new shared services pool could involve Patty and others in crafting this new role with an eye toward making it as meaningful as possible. These five steps would have cost little, but they would have made the change easier for Patty and strengthened the overall adaptability of the system.

Without compassion, workplaces can become powerful amplifiers of human suffering. This book offers a fuller picture of how to create organizations that awaken compassion. First we define the key concepts and establish the case for compassion. The next part of the book focuses on individuals at work, and is designed to help you understand the four aspects of the compassion process more deeply and identify skills you can use to increase compassion in your work, no matter what it is. The third part of the book focuses on organizations. It is designed to help you become a compassion architect for your organization, explaining a framework for understanding and designing a social architecture that enables compassion. The fourth part of the book presents tools that bring all the ideas together and helps you apply them to awaken compassion in your own work life and across your organization.

2

DOES COMPASSION
AT WORK
REALLY MATTER?

IT'S NOT ALWAYS OBVIOUS TO businesspeople, immersed in competitive markets or dealing with financial bottom-line questions, that compassion is relevant to their world. For employees who are under strain from deadlines or the stress of living up to performance demands, it's easy to forget that something that seems "soft" like compassion is significant. Facing challenges from turbulent environments, regulatory changes, or customer complaints, leaders and managers can easily dismiss the need for compassion. But when seeking to build high-performing organizations that meet the challenges of a twenty-first-century work environment, compassion matters more than most people recognize.

Sometimes people think that compassion obviously matters in a not-for-profit setting driven by a mission that relates to helping. Not so. While the rhetoric of compassion might be more recognized in these organizations, the same strain, stress, and demands for change, coupled with a lack of resources, can make it easy for

13

people to overlook the value of compassion in their day-to-day work. Similarly in health care, where compassion is at the heart of the professional value system, we see that the practice of compassion at work is often driven out by overload, time pressure, technological changes, financial worries, regulatory mandates, and other organizational pressures that make humanistic concerns seem marginal.

It's time to challenge this tendency to disregard the value of compassion. We articulate a strategic case for the fundamental value of compassion that emerges from evidence gathered by a number of researchers across a range of disciplines. While a growing body of research continues to highlight new benefits, significant questions about the fundamental value of compassion for organizations have been answered. Compassion is an irreplaceable dimension of excellence for any organization that wants to make the most of its human capabilities.

COMPASSION TIPS THE BOTTOM LINE

Our colleague Kim Cameron has spent the last decade examining the impact of what he calls the *virtuousness* of an organization on its financial and operational performance. By virtuousness, Kim means characteristics or strengths that represent the best of the human condition and the highest aspirations of human beings. Kim's research shows that compassion as part of the values of an organization makes a measurable difference in productivity and financial performance. In a study of eighteen organizations that had recently engaged in downsizing, the extent to which employees characterized their organizations as more virtuous was correlated with higher profitability, greater productivity, and enhanced customer retention.[1] Another study examined performance over two years across forty business units in the financial services industry. When compassion was part of the values of the business unit, as rated by the members, the compassionate units exhibited better financial performance, executives perceived the compassionate units as more effective, and these units realized higher employee and customer retention.[2]

Studies that examine compassion as an overall characteristic of organizations are still rare. Even so, strong evidence emerges from unexpected sources. For instance, when members of American organizations were surveyed after the terrorist attacks of September 11, 2001, employees who rated their workplaces as excellent at offering compassion in the wake of the crisis became far more engaged in their work. On the other hand, when people felt that their organizations did not value compassion in the wake of the attacks, more than a third of members became actively disengaged, meaning that they were likely causing harm to their workplaces. This finding led Gallup researchers to caution top leaders: "When compassion is called for, know that your bottom line is at stake."[3]

COMPASSION FUELS STRATEGIC ADVANTAGE

Organizational strategy scholars write about strategic advantage as being driven by the *collective capabilities* of organizations. By collective capability we refer to a group's ability to collectively undertake action to do something important for the organization, such as creatively innovating products or quickly changing services in response to customer feedback. Compassion is at the heart of an organization's ability to do these things. Because of its role in enhancing collective capabilities like innovation, service quality, collaboration, and adaptability, compassion matters for competitive advantage. Think of it this way: when human suffering threatens to diminish collective capabilities such as working together creatively and quickly, compassion restores and even strengthens the organization's ability to accomplish its aims. For this reason, compassion belongs on every leader's strategic agenda.

Compassion makes strategic advantages more sustainable. Sustainable strategic success matters for all organizations, regardless of their sector or industry. Capabilities that cannot be easily substituted or imitated—such as service infused with compassion and care—are particularly advantageous over the long term.[4] Consider the example set by the Ritz-Carlton hotel chain. To sustain its strategic advantage based in excellent individualized service, the Ritz needs people who can build high-quality connections with customers and respond to their suffering with compassion. In a story told by Gallup researchers, an employee at the Ritz provided a scented candle for a guest who had experienced a particularly stressful travel hassle and arrived just before an important meeting, bedraggled and exhausted.[5] Feeling this gesture as an act of compassion, the guest complimented the employee and the hotel. When managers in the hotel learned how much she appreciated this act of compassion, they alerted the entire Ritz system and arranged for a scented candle to be placed in her room on every visit. She became an extremely loyal Ritz customer, because she felt that the organization cared about her. These seemingly small actions are what we call compassion moves in chapter 6; compassion moves like this are the fuel for a sustainable competitive service advantage. Research shows that employees can more easily build high-quality connections like this when they experience compassion in their own work teams[6] and when they are encouraged to express compassion for their customers.[7]

The same general link between collective capability and compassion is true for other hard-to-imitate human-based capabilities, not just hospitality. Let's look at six capabilities that have repercussions for almost every organization's strategic success: innovation, service quality, collaboration, recruiting and retaining talented people, employee and customer engagement, and adaptability to changing environments. We can find compassion at the heart of each.

KEY POINTS: THE COMPASSION ADVANTAGE

∞ Compassion contributes to an organization's financial resilience, profitability, and customer retention after downsizing.

∞ Compassionate business units exhibit better financial performance and higher employee and customer retention.

∞ Compassion fuels human-based collective capabilities such as creativity and learning that contribute to sustainable competitive advantage.

∞ Compassion matters for six types of strategic advantage that have repercussions for all organizations: innovation, service quality, collaboration, retaining talented people, employee and customer engagement, and adaptability to change.

COMPASSION AND INNOVATION

Generating new products, services, processes, and ideas is a deeply human activity. Acting on creative ideas to put them into production or operation is the cornerstone of an innovation capability. Evidence indicates that compassion in organizations bolsters human creativity and the capability for innovation in two ways—first, by motivating new ideas, and second, by creating psychological safety that enhances learning.

COMPASSION MOTIVATES INNOVATION

When an organization's purpose is linked to alleviating suffering, the call for compassion in people's work can stimulate human creativity that fuels innovation. Nina Simosko is a Silicon Valley executive who spends a good deal of time wondering about what keeps technology companies on the forefront of innovation. "I've come to learn that people come to work searching for purpose and meaning, much as they do in their everyday lives," she writes. "Frankly, if they come to believe that the company's sole mission is to make money for shareholders, people don't find that terribly attractive."[8] A purpose that fuels innovation doesn't have to be as grandiose as ending world poverty, but it does have to be human-centered and directed toward alleviating suffering.

Putting compassion directly in the center of this kind of innovation is motivating. For instance, FoodLab is an entrepreneurial organization that was studied by our colleague Suntae Kim, one of a number of scholars who are investigating compassion in the field of social entrepreneurship.[9] FoodLab explicitly seeks to reduce suffering created by hunger and lack of access to fresh, local, healthy food in urban Detroit. In Suntae's studies of social entrepreneurs in Detroit, all of the founders of social ventures were motivated to start a business as a means for alleviating suffering in their communities.

Compassion can motivate innovation in the design process as well. Powerful new ideas are often the result of empathic designs created in collaboration with users. Interaction with users can help designers to take their perspective and draw out feelings of concern for their experience. Empathy equips innovation teams with ideas for products and services that alleviate suffering, expanding the organization's effectiveness and customer base.[10]

An example of compassion motivating the innovation of a business model and products comes from Dr. Govindappa Venkataswamy, who founded an eye clinic out of his family home in South India at the age of 58, with little money and no business plan. Dr. V, as he became known around the world, famously wondered why, when the McDonald's Corporation could accomplish highly consistent, reliable, and clear standards for hamburgers in restaurants all around the world, couldn't the same be done for eye surgeries? This curious link between hamburgers and health care in Dr. V's mind grew into a counterintuitive experiment to offer high-volume eye surgery in a clinic that charged whatever patients could afford to pay. Dr. V's clinic grew as his high-volume, low-cost surgical model took off. Aravind's surgeons each perform more than 2,000 surgeries a year, compared with only a few hundred for each US physician, while treating one-third of patients at no charge. In 2011, Aravind clinics saw seventy-five hundred patients each day, performed 850 to 1,000 surgeries, and manufactured thousands of components for eye surgery while holding daily classes for more than four hundred professionals who visited hoping to learn from their model.

Along with this operational success, Aravind is also a financial success. Because of its impeccable attention to quality and detail, Aravind attracts not only poor patients who can afford to pay little but also thousands who pay full price for comprehensive specialty care. Aravind now operates at a surplus. When scholars have tried to unpack how Aravind became one of the lowest-cost, highest-quality eye care systems in the world, they found compassion as a primary driver of innovation. Pavithra Mehta and Suchitra Shenoy, who wrote a book about the Aravind business model, conclude: "Aravind is an unconventional model that came into being not despite but because of the deep-seated compassion at its core."[11]

COMPASSION FOSTERS LEARNING

The second way in which compassion fuels a strategic advantage based on innovation involves its role in learning. Harvard scholar Amy Edmondson has been on the forefront of developing a fresh understanding of the role of compassion in fueling innovation through its impact on learning. In an early study, Amy observed the work of eight different hospital units, each of which seemed different to observers in terms of its quality of teamwork.[12] She expected that the units with the best teamwork would also have the lowest rates of medical errors. When she analyzed the data, however, she found exactly the opposite. The units that seemed the most supportive and scored highest on a survey of team performance had the *highest* rates of errors. Determined to understand this counterintuitive result, Amy dug deeper.

She gathered new data that showed that detecting and reporting medical errors is complex. What counts as an error isn't always clear. Lots of errors are never registered in any official database. What are called "near misses," when a team intercepts an error before it affects a patient, were almost never logged. In the teams with less teamwork and less trust, people didn't report errors unless they absolutely had to do so. These teams rarely talked about errors or what they could learn from them. They looked the other way if they saw coworkers fail. Contrast this with the units with more teamwork. They exhibited what Amy called *psychological safety*—a willingness to discuss and learn from errors, failures, mistakes, or near misses. They reported errors more often and talked about them more easily.[13] They also learned more and were more innovative. Compassion helps people to greet errors and failures with the open-mindedness and open-heartedness that foster learning.

COMPASSION AND SERVICE QUALITY

As we were writing this chapter, Monica's beloved Bernese mountain dog, Amaia, was gravely ill with cancer. Monica had planned to take the dog to a specialty veterinary treatment center in another city and had booked a hotel nearby. On the eve of her arrival, she got news that Amaia's tumor was not treatable. Monica recounted, "I called the booking service I had used for the hotel room and informed the agent that I would no longer need the reservation."

"I see that you are subject to a 100 percent cancellation charge at this time," the agent said.

"That's OK, I understand," Monica answered. "I just wanted you to be aware that I won't be checking in." The agent asked why she was canceling the reservation.

"I was going to take my dog for treatment at the specialty hospital near the hotel, but . . ." Monica felt tears welling up in her eyes and her voice wavered. Taking a deep breath, she described the situation.

"I'm so sorry," the reservation agent responded genuinely. "Let me at least call the hotel and see what we can do." About a half hour later, Monica received an email from the reservation service. The agent wrote:

> Thank you for contacting us.
>
> I am so sorry to hear about your pet. As we discussed during our phone conversation, I approached the hotel on your behalf and asked them to cancel your reservation without any penalties. I am happy to confirm that the request has been approved.
>
> I am glad to have helped. I am so sorry for what you are going through.

Though Monica's phone call was a momentary interaction, just one of many in this call center employee's day, the agent really listened. Instead of treating this as just another transaction, the reservation agent tuned in to Monica's sadness and responded with compassion. Research by the Gallup organization shows that genuine expressions of compassion such as this one, when delivered authentically as part of high-quality service, create brand loyalty and forge lasting bonds with customers.[14] That was certainly Monica's feeling about the booking service and her intentions to use it again in the future. It was as if she had received a gift.

Research supports the idea that when employees give feelings and actions as gifts to customers, not only does the customer become more loyal, but the employee feels better about work as well. In Monica's case, the reservation agent's quick follow-up, with a personal expression of care, represents what some researchers have called a *philanthropic approach to emotions* at work.[15] This kind of approach highlights the ability of service providers to give feelings and actions freely at their own initiative as gifts to their customers in order to express empathy and compassion. The connections formed through a philanthropic approach to emotions at work can be rewarding and motivating.[16]

This approach contrasts with an emphasis on emotional labor, where employees like flight attendants must smile and act cordially toward even the rudest of customers, expressing emotions that they don't actually feel in order to perform their work. Research shows that emotional labor can be draining and contribute to burnout.[17] This reinforces the idea that compassion at work can't be mandated—instead it emerges when people authentically pick up on suffering and feel moved to respond.

Service work is often measured in time to resolution or other metrics that create pressure to shut down encounters with clients quickly. Managers and leaders who are striving to deliver distinctive high-quality service that fuels strategic advantage must recognize that there are times when employees who interact with customers who are suffering will want to give their customers time and attention as a kind of gift. Making room for compassion as part of a service strategy opens the door for employees to have a more philan-thropic approach to their interactions. Great benefits accrue to the employee when work is more genuinely compassionate, and to the organization in customers' loyalty and an inclination to recommend the service to others.

COMPASSION AND COLLABORATION

Complex organizations need people who coordinate and collaborate across all kinds of boundaries. Divisions proliferate in organizations, whether from different forms of expertise, a variety of professional norms and education, different parts of supply chains, geographic and time boundaries, or cultural differences, just to name a few. When we think about coordination and collaboration across boundaries like these, research highlights the importance of volun-tary actions that people undertake to work with others for shared advantage or mutual benefit.[18] This goes beyond simply working together on tasks. Coordination and collaboration are domains in which qualities of human relationships determine strategic success.

Important evidence related to the impact of compassion on coordination and collaboration comes from the work of organiza-tional scholar Jody Hoffer Gittell.[19] Her research has addressed a central strategic question in the airline industry: when short-haul flights are inherently more expensive for the airline to operate than long-haul flights, how was it possible for Southwest Airlines to be-come the leading low-cost airline in the United States? As with the Aravind eye clinic in India, where we saw compassion at the heart of shaking up the entire production logic of an industry, compassion is hidden at the heart of Southwest's story as well. In this case, com-passion infuses rapid coordination with respect, trust, and strong human connections.

One key to Southwest's strategic advantage is its capability for quick turnarounds at airline gates. It's not an exaggeration to say that at Southwest Airlines, cooperation is money. As employees learn quickly, "Our planes don't make any money sitting on the ground—we have to get them back into the air."[20] An aircraft turn-around involves coordination among twelve different functional roles, from pilots and crew to ticketing and gate agents to multiple maintenance, baggage, and cargo functions. Plenty of factors make coordination difficult. Differences in status can sometimes hinder willingness to engage in communication. Each function works in a different geographical area of the airport, providing little access to one another. Each function holds distinctive expertise about a part of the process, which may or may not be valued by other functions. Each function has distinct labor practices, different measures against which they judge their work, and different professional norms and values. In most airlines, cooperation between these functions isn't generally warm. But within Southwest, a sense of egalitarianism pervades the organization, supporting a value of caring for one another that fuels cooperation across all these boundaries. Compassion in the coordination process becomes key to strategic success that hinges on this type of seamlessly coordinated effort.

Jody's findings, now referred to in a theory of *relational coordination*, demonstrate significant positive effects of the kind of compassion that supports coordination. In sixty-nine studies across sixteen different industries and eighteen different countries, relational coordination has been shown to be essential to better financial performance, efficiency, quality, and safety.[21] Compassion is at the heart of transformative cooperation.[22]

COMPASSION AND TALENT

Doing any kind of great work requires great people. Finding them and keeping them is central to any human-based strategic advantage. Building compassion into recruiting and hiring helps organizations find talented employees with the right cultural fit, which matters more than ever.[23] Experiencing compassion as part of the work environment also builds commitment, which helps organizations keep talented people.

Some organizations with compassion at their core deliberately emphasize compassion during the recruiting and hiring process. At the social media firm LinkedIn, for instance, the organization as a whole values the idea of compassionate management, and the CEO, Jeff Weiner, routinely speaks about this value in public.[24] We will talk more about compassion and leaders in chapter 10. In relation to recruiting at LinkedIn, we documented the case of a hiring manager who has adapted his interview process based on the values that Jeff Weiner espouses. He routinely asks candidates to tell him what they would do if they were just about to step into leadership of a very important global meeting and they got the news that a valued employee at a different location had been rushed to the hospital.[25] There's no correct answer to the question, but a candidate's responses help him to understand the candidate's potential fit with the organization's culture. Our research also shows that experiences of compassion—giving it, receiving it, and even witnessing it at work—are significantly related to commitment and employees' intentions to stay with their organizations.[26] In the recipe for developing sustainable competitive advantage through people, compassion is a surprise ingredient.

COMPASSION AND ENGAGEMENT

Organizations need people who are actively involved in and en-thusiastic about their work, the essence of employee engagement. Measures of the engagement of employees are significant predictors of an organization's overall profitability and productivity.[27] Since the late 1990s, the Gallup organization has surveyed more than twenty-five million employees in 195 countries, finding that engaged employees also tend to create engaged customers who are involved in and enthusiastic about an organization's products or services.

Compassion is hidden at the heart of employee engagement. One group of questions on the engagement survey asks about the quality of relationships at work and whether supervisors or others "care about me as a person." As we've already seen, caring relation-ships at work are a source of intrinsic motivation. Research shows that people want to care about others at work, and will volunteer or seek out opportunities to engage with compassion.[28] In our research, we met Isabel, whose story illuminates the relationship between compassion and employee engagement. Isabel told us that when she was diagnosed with and treated for breast cancer, she "was flooded with hugs, prayers, gifts, and tons of support throughout the various surgeries and chemotherapy. I was so overwhelmed when food was delivered to my house to feed my family by this group of very caring people from work. I have never felt so loved. This ex-perience has given me a deeper commitment to my coworkers, and I find myself contributing to all other calls for sharing and giving." In Isabel's story we see how an experience of receiving compassion from coworkers translated into increased engagement at work. And in terms of strategic success, Gallup's research shows: "Engaged employees create engaged customers, and those engaged customers spend more money, more often with their preferred brands."[29]

COMPASSION AND ADAPTABILITY

An organization must have the capacity to perform with excellence at the same time that it adapts to fluctuating markets, changing competitive landscapes, advancing technologies, shifting regulatory environments, and emerging social or environmental conditions. Adaptability to change is at the heart of sustaining strategic competitive advantage over time. It has become a truism that change is a constant in organizational life. Even so, the difficulty and pain associated with change often goes unaddressed—and these are missed opportunities for compassion at work. As we saw in Patty's story in chapter I, when organizational change opens the door to suffering, greeting change with compassion is an underrecognized strategy for enhancing an organization's adaptability.[30]

Organizational researchers Karen Golden-Biddle and Jina Mao quote from the former CEO of a health organization, who described the visceral sense of suffering that sometimes accompanies organizational change: "I can remember a conversation with my new boss . . . it was a conversation around goals—where we were headed. And I said that, as I look over my shoulder at the change that had occurred in the region, I see *all these human remains strewn in the ditches*."[31] When this is our experience of organizational change, it's obvious that compassion is necessary and valuable. Karen and Jina show that leaders and managers who notice suffering, relate with empathy and concern, and actively attend to emotions, make change easier. People affected by change done with compassion are less likely to resist and more likely to invest in making change effective.[32]

Compassion researcher Donde Ashmos Plowman and her colleagues showed how an urban church that was in severe decline enlisted creative ideas from its members in hopes of shifting the downward trend in financial resources and membership.[33] Compassion for the organization's broader community of stakeholders sparked ideas about new services the church could offer, including breakfast for homeless urban residents in the neighborhood. As these sparks of change caught fire in the organization, change accelerated because new people added new ideas that expanded the pattern of compassion. For instance, a doctor volunteered medical services to be offered during the breakfasts. More ideas caught on. Soon the church offered meal services, a full clinic, showers, employment services, and more. The organization reversed its decline. Its adaptability was fueled almost entirely by sparks of compassion that ignited passion for change.

KEY POINTS: HOW COMPASSION BUILDS COMPETITIVE ADVANTAGES

∞ Compassion fuels innovation by motivating creative ideas and by fostering psychological safety that enables learning.

∞ Compassion fuels service quality by motivating a philanthropic approach to emotions, building customer loyalty.

∞ Compassion fuels collaboration by building trust and respect that increase people's willingness and ability to work together for mutual benefit.

∞ Compassion fuels the recruiting and retaining of talented people by increasing commitment and cultural fit.

∞ Compassion fuels employee and customer engagement by helping people to feel cared about at work.

∞ Compassion fuels adaptability by alleviating the pain caused by change processes and sparking passion that motivates resourceful change.

■ AN INVITATION TO REFLECT ON THE CASE FOR COMPASSION

Technologies will race onward. Robotics will replace human labor, creating even more change in the future of work.[34] Organizations will need to adapt and to create things that have never existed before. When organizations need adaptability and innovation, they also need human ingenuity—the kind of ingenuity that can be crushed by unmet grief or pain at work.[35] In this way, compassion is at the heart of success.

Some organizations succeed because they offer high-touch services that respond to the unpredictable desires and demands of clients. These organizations require the sensitivity and responsiveness of people who can harness empathy and compassion to deliver great service. All organizations do what they do because they can find and keep people who engage with work. Human-based capabilities require compassion.

More and more organizations strive to work together in ways that are unprecedented, where partnerships can make or break success. These forms of strategic advantage depend on people who can coordinate and collaborate for mutual benefit. People who can compassionately notice and respectfully embrace one another's states of mind and heart propel or undermine this form of competitive advantage. Compassion is not just a nice-to-have; it is the hidden heart of strategic success.

How does compassion comprise the hidden heart of strategic advantage in your organization?

PART TWO

AWAKENING COMPASSION IN OUR WORK LIVES

It's easy to overlook, but suffering is everywhere in organizations —from the tiniest workplace to the largest. Alongside it comes the possibility of awakening compassion at work. Just today, on Monica's ride to the airport on a business trip, a conversation with the taxi driver that had begun as a casual discussion evoked an unusual revelation about suffering. It turned out that the driver's estranged wife lived in the city that Monica was going to visit, and the conversation prompted him to reflect on the depth of loneliness in his life and how much he missed being with his children. Even in a workplace of *one*, like this taxi, suffering surfaces in unexpected ways when a connection with a client evokes painful memories or brings a sense of loneliness into view.

Like the driver who had a choice about how much suffering to reveal, Monica faced a choice as well. Would she pay attention, given the other distractions she faced embarking on a business trip? Would she listen in a way that suspended judgment and led to empathy and concern, or look the other way in the face of such strong emotion from a stranger? Would she respond with words of comfort or hesitate to act for fear of not knowing what to say? These are the interpersonal moments and choices that make up compassion in our work lives.

Most of us don't toil in workplaces of one, however. The opportunities for suffering at work multiply with the size and complexity of organizations, as do the obstacles to giving voice to suffering as part of work life. Brutal deadlines, competitive pressure, insensitive management, toxic work cultures, relentless schedules and demands—these create a cocktail that is especially potent for amplifying human suffering. Add a dash of a culture that makes silence about emotions normative or attaches a hint of stigma to pain at work, and we have a recipe for workplaces that undermine compassion.

The next chapters explore each of the four aspects of compassion —*noticing, interpreting, feeling,* and *acting*—explaining what is involved personally and interpersonally. We take a close look at how the work environment shapes what we as individuals notice, think, feel, and do. The premise is that with a deeper understanding of compassion and a heightened awareness of the factors around us that influence it, each of us can increase our day-to-day experience of compassion at work. In fact, these everyday "micro moves" are often where compassion most strongly abides in people's experience. Even if we cannot change large elements in the organization like leadership or culture, Finnish compassion researcher Anne Birgitta Pessi reminds us that when it comes to compassion, "small is all."[1]

3

NOTICING: THE PORTAL TO AWAKENING COMPASSION

SUFFERING THAT ISN'T NOTICED will never be met with compassion. That is why noticing is the portal to awakening compassion at work. At first glance, noticing seems simple. But we have found that paying attention to suffering in work environments is much harder than it seems.

We uncovered a compelling example of the complexities of noticing as a portal to compassion when we studied Dorothy's organization. When Dorothy's husband was diagnosed with kidney failure, she asked for time off to be with him in the hospital. Thinking it would be just a few days, Dorothy, a clerk at an insurance company, didn't notify anyone about why she needed the time off. The organization prided itself on its financial and managerial discipline, and Dorothy was a no-nonsense employee who had always been on time and on budget. But three weeks later, Dorothy was on the edge of being terminated for too many absences and late arrivals. The company's strict attendance and tardiness policy meant that each absence over an approved number earned Dorothy a point in the system, and after five points in a year, dismissal was mandatory. She had quickly racked up four and half points before she decided to talk to her manager. She couldn't remember the last time she had even earned a point in the system. She didn't know what to say. She felt ashamed, and she didn't want to lose the job.

Feelings of shame or fear can easily lead people to withhold information about suffering at work, blocking compassion. For people attuned to suffering at work, any knock on the door can be an invitation to compassion. Dorothy's manager Sandeep invited her to come in and sit down. "I don't know what to do," Dorothy blurted out almost immediately, flushed with embarrassment. Sandeep picked up on this as a clue that perhaps suffering was surfacing. People often offer clues, if we are paying attention. Sometime they are not as engaged as usual. Sometimes their bodies convey exhaustion or tension. Sometimes their facial expressions display sadness or anger. Noticing suffering at work is partly learning how to pick up on these clues and work with them. In fact, researcher Max Bazerman equates becoming a great leader with becoming "a first-class noticer."[1] While we don't often conceptualize it this way, noticing is a skill that we can build with awareness and practice.

Sandeep had already noticed Dorothy's unusual absences, and his attention was heightened further because the organizational attendance system had flagged her as being in danger of dismissal. "You haven't been acting like yourself," Sandeep observed. He said it with kindness, but his comment was direct. When Dorothy stayed quiet, he said gently, "It might help us both if I could understand why."

NOTICING THROUGH INQUIRY WORK

Sandeep's question acted as a portal to compassion at work. Dorothy's shame and fear had prevented her from reaching out or asking for help. When people do not reveal what is happening in their lives, often suffering surfaces because someone like Sandeep notices behavior outside of a usual pattern and asks about it. Our CompassionLab colleague Reut Livne-Tarandach calls systematic questions that flow from curiosity about the suffering of another person *inquiry work*. Inquiry work helps us notice suffering because it requires being willing to ask about what someone is experiencing instead of assuming that his or her experience is similar to our own. In her study of how people lead and manage a summer camp for children whose parents have cancer, Reut finds that camp counselors and campers themselves are more effective in responding to suffering that surfaces at camp when they remain curious. Campers and counselors use questions to draw out more information about one another's state of mind and heart, using inquiry work as a skilled form of noticing that opens space for compassion. Developing both a comfort and a vocabulary to ask humble, gentle, and kind questions about someone's experience is another aspect of skillful noticing that we can learn.[2]

Sandeep's invitation for Dorothy to talk about what was happening is an example of skillful noticing through inquiry work. His observation that Dorothy wasn't acting like herself brackets this period in Dorothy's work from her prior performance, reinforcing Dorothy's value as an employee. Sandeep's curiosity told Dorothy, not just in words but also through his facial expressions, voice, posture in the chair, eye contact, and attentive presence, that he was present with her and was open to her situation.

As we said, noticing suffering at work is harder than we might assume—both for the person suffering, who risks drawing attention to herself, like Dorothy, and for the person who risks asking a question that opens up an unknown topic, like Sandeep. Part of what makes noticing suffering more difficult than we expect it to be is that suffering is related to larger personal questions about meaning and existence. In fact, a definition of suffering is experience that threatens our sense of holistic integrity and existence.[3] For Dorothy, her husband's illness evoked larger questions about mortality, while the need to care for him threatened her sense of integrity at work. Sometimes the existential questions tied to suffering become frightening or overwhelming, blocking both our ability to reveal suffering and our willingness to notice and inquire. This fundamental difficulty is another reason that noticing suffering is more difficult than we might imagine in work organizations.

It is also the case that suffering in our current experience takes on meaning in relation to our past experiences. If we haven't experienced a form of suffering, it is sometimes hard to notice its subtle implications. We have found that someone who can relate to a similar source of suffering in his or her past is often attuned to picking up on small clues and inquiring in ways that open up space for suffering to surface. For instance, in our study of an organization's response to people who lost everything in a fire, we found that people who had experienced fires or natural disasters were better at noticing some aspects of this form of suffering. This means that different coworkers will notice different things about one another. Workplaces can use this distributed noticing by taking advantage of communication and ties between people in social networks so that clues related to suffering are shared. We will pick up on this systemic aspect of attention in the third section of the book.

Finally, the meaning of suffering differs across cultures and times of life, which is another reason that it can be difficult for us to notice. Philosopher Elaine Scarry has written that the very nature of suffering is inexpressibility, meaning that the experience of suffering and what it means to us are almost impossible to adequately convey to others.[4] In that way, we are all like Dorothy and Sandeep—the one who suffers is mute, and the one who notices must be able to inquire and help give voice to pain. Noticing suffering involves figuring out together how to say the unsayable.

KEY POINTS: NOTICING THROUGH INQUIRY WORK

- ∞ Noticing suffering at work is harder than we expect.
- ∞ When suffering goes unnoticed in organizations, compassion fails.
- ∞ Suffering is inherently difficult to express. Sometimes feelings of shame, fear, or uncertainty will make it even more difficult.
- ∞ Sometimes people notice suffering by drawing on a similar experience from their past.
- ∞ Noticing becomes more likely and skilled as we learn how to discern people's patterns of energy and engagement and pick up on deviations from those patterns.
- ∞ We can build skill in noticing by learning to ask gentle, humble questions about others' experiences. This is called *inquiry work*, and it is crucial to awakening compassion.

ORGANIZATIONS SHAPE WHAT WE NOTICE

Suffering often hides in other forms of work behavior that mask its influence, as in Dorothy's case, where suffering was manifest by tardiness and absence from work. Her behavior could be perceived as inadequate performance, but it was actually being driven by distractions from suffering and caregiving. This happens often, especially when people who feel shame or for other reasons desire privacy for their personal lives withhold information about illness, hardship, loss, or grief that is impacting their work performance in some way. Organizations can make it harder to notice suffering that is masquerading as performance deficits. Typical policies that govern attendance, tardiness, dress code, and other aspects of workplace discipline tend to focus us on punishment. We notice the rule being broken instead of the person behind the rule.

In Dorothy's workplace, with its values of discipline and order, her inability to live up to the rigid time demands triggered concern about punishment. Dorothy, as a no-nonsense, responsible employee, felt that the missed work time that came from her need to tend to her husband's illness was irresponsible. The punishing tone of the attendance rules and their emphasis on dismissal exacerbated Dorothy's personal self-criticism and internal shame. Her worry about being irresponsible prompted her to hide her circumstances, making it even more difficult for others to notice what was happening and intervene. Many organizational policies, procedures, rules, goals, and norms shape what we pay attention to and how we regard deviations from it. At times, organizational factors can help us notice something unusual—such as when the system flagged Sandeep about Dorothy's attendance irregularities. But without attention to suffering and his skilled inquiry work,

Sandeep could simply have used the flag to scold Dorothy or even fire her rather than to awaken compassion.

When Sandeep learned that Dorothy's husband had experienced kidney failure and was undergoing continuous treatment, her absences and lateness made a new kind of sense to him. When he also learned that Dorothy was hopeful that her husband would have transplant surgery but the organ could arrive at any moment, Sandeep paid attention to Dorothy's agitation in a new way. Her need for greater flexibility than the attendance policy allowed was obvious to him. Sandeep wanted to keep a good employee, not lose her to an arbitrary attendance count. He called his human resources partner and obtained a waiver for the points that Dorothy had earned on days when her husband was hospitalized. With the burden of imminent termination lifted, Dorothy felt flooded with gratitude. Her commitment to her work deepened even further. Sandeep's attention and his compassionate response to Dorothy's life circumstances alleviated some of her suffering and at the same time enabled the organization to retain a valuable employee.

SPREADING ATTENTION TO SUFFERING

Often it is quiet conversations in a conference room or a manager's office that awaken compassion, just as with Sandeep and Dorothy. These interpersonal moments direct our attention to suffering that would otherwise go unnoticed. Instances when suffering surfaces between two people become opportunities for activating the attention of others who can also respond.

In Dorothy and Sandeep's case, after the immediate threat to Dorothy's employment had been addressed, Sandeep's attention could have wavered. As an experienced manager, however, Sandeep knew that this was just the beginning of Dorothy's need for compassion. Her husband's illness would be protracted, and the transplant opportunity might interrupt Dorothy's attendance again at any time. Sandeep asked Dorothy if he could tell others about what she was going through. This is an important aspect of noticing and spreading attention to suffering: gaining permission about what can be shared.

Reluctantly, Dorothy agreed. Talking to Sandeep helped her see that revealing her circumstances would make it easier for others to help if she had to be absent or late in the future. With her permission, Sandeep began to mention Dorothy's husband's illness to others in the organization. He invited others with ideas of how to support Dorothy to meet with him. Attention began to spread, feeding a river of compassion. As word spread, coworkers found a new clarity about why Dorothy had been acting strangely. This spurred them toward the rest of the process—interpreting, feeling, and acting with compassion. One member of Sandeep's team who knew Dorothy as a neighbor outside of work volunteered to check in with Dorothy each morning to monitor her husband's status on the transplant list. This helped Dorothy to more easily relay information when she needed to be unexpectedly absent, preventing her from accruing points in the system unnecessarily. Others on her team tracked her tasks on a weekly basis, so that they could easily pick up her workload whenever the transplant call came. This gave both Dorothy and her coworkers peace of mind about a potential bottleneck in the organization's performance.

Attention spread beyond their immediate group. Someone outside of Sandeep's unit organized a nonprofit fund into which anyone could make financial donations to help Dorothy and her husband pay the mounting medical bills. He knew firsthand of the need for this, having been driven almost to the point of bankruptcy when his wife died of cancer. As the attention to Dorothy's life circumstances spread throughout the organization, the attention brought with it new forms of compassion. Little had she understood that by withholding her situation from her manager and coworkers, Dorothy had also inadvertently denied them all this opportunity to relate with compassion.

KEY POINTS: ORGANIZATIONS SHAPE
ATTENTION TO SUFFERING

- ∞ Time pressure, overload, and performance demands distract us from noticing suffering at work.
- ∞ Policies, rules, and norms of conduct can orient us toward punishment rather than curiosity about what is happening with the person.
- ∞ Ask for permission to share a coworker's life circumstances if you learn about suffering. Spread attention to awaken compassion.
- ∞ As attention to suffering spreads, new ideas about how to respond also come to the surface.

AN INVITATION TO REFLECT ON NOTICING AS A PORTAL TO COMPASSION

In the flow of daily work life, colliding people and activities create a form of surface tension—that mystery of physics that allows water sliders to glide across the top of ponds. The surface tension of work allows everyone to glide across the seemingly solid surface. But mysteriously, maybe with a knock on a manager's door, the surface that allowed life to seem ordinary is breached. Suffering breaks through.

When suffering surfaces this way in work life, the sudden shift from a task-focused conversation to the existential questions that come along with loss or grief or illness can be jarring or even frightening. To awaken compassion, we can learn how to engage in skilled inquiry work that makes room for these sorts of revelations. We can learn to keep our eyes open for changes in people's usual patterns. We can find a way together to give voice to suffering. We can learn to ask for permission to share people's circumstances, trusting that as attention to suffering spreads, so does compassion.

∞

Is there a moment when suffering broke the surface tension of everyday work and you were called on to inquire about another person's pain? Recognizing that noticing suffering is a portal, do you also see instances in which you may have overlooked suffering at work? What do these reflections show you about awakening compassion in your work?

INTERPRETING: THE KEY TO RESPONDING WITH COMPASSION

WE CREATED A "FOUND POEM" composed from the words of interview participants who were describing experiences of compassion at work. In it, people described common assumptions that made interpreting suffering difficult, such as:

> There was a real norm in our department of modesty and
> always presenting a good face.
>
> Keep your skeletons at home.
>
> You're not supposed to have a personal life.
>
> You're supposed to take care of business.[1]

Work organizations that have widespread and pervasive assumptions about putting on a good face or keeping our skeletons at home make it harder to understand suffering. These assumptions dispose us to interpret suffering as unworthy of compassion at work. If we can't interpret suffering in a way that makes sense and calls up feelings of concern, compassion falters. It is only when we understand another person's suffering as real and worthy that we include him or her in our circle of concern. While these interpretations might seem straightforward, they warrant a closer look as a key to responding with compassion.

THREE INTERPRETATIONS THAT CLOSE DOWN COMPASSION

Compassion researchers who investigate interpretations focus on what they call "appraisals" of suffering, which are accounts that we use to explain the causes of suffering to ourselves and others.[2] Appraisals are pivotal. We make them at lightning speed. Our brains jump to these interpretations so quickly that the process may be invisible to us.[3] For example, recall a moment when you thought to yourself about someone else: "You made this mess; now you have to suffer the consequences!" When we construe someone as blameworthy, that's the first kind of appraisal that shuts down compassion. Researchers show us that we feel less empathy and concern when we determine that someone is responsible for his or her own suffering.

The next type of interpretation that closes down compassion comes about when we jump to the conclusion that someone doesn't deserve our concern. Often these interpretations are swayed by stereotypes or stigmas. For instance, recall a time when someone who seemed homeless or otherwise impoverished asked you for money, and the thought passed through your mind, "If he'd just get a job, he wouldn't have to be begging on the street." Whether or not it's true, this type of interpretation shuts down compassion.

The third type of interpretation involves how we understand our own capacity to respond when someone who is suffering really needs something. If we jump to the quick conclusion that we don't have the resources or the capacity to respond, the compassion process shuts down. Recall a time when you said to yourself, "I just can't handle this right now!" That interpretation of the situation makes you less likely to act with compassion.

As we said, these interpretations happen at the speed of thought, so they color compassion every time we encounter suffering. Many factors play into our largely automatic interpretations like these, including work experience, training, organizational culture, heritage, national culture, family traditions, position in the organization, and the implicit biases that we develop simply by internalizing stereotypes propagated by social systems.[4] For instance, compassion researcher Dan Martin and his colleagues have demonstrated that when students choose business or law as a major in college, with the logic of succeeding economically, these students are significantly more likely to internalize economic stereotypes about people in lower social classes as being innately inferior.[5] This orientation to the world becomes an obstacle to compassion. Sociologist Candace Clark has documented a widespread cultural assumption in the United States that if people are suffering from poverty or financial need, we are likely to blame them for their suffering, because Americans interpret that those in poverty just aren't willing to work hard enough.[6] We all carry around these internalized cultural assumptions about suffering. Recognizing them, challenging them in ourselves, and becoming more aware of how to change them is key to awakening compassion at work.

MORE GENEROUS INTERPRETATIONS
OF SUFFERING

We can use this research that shows us how interpretations shut down compassion to likewise understand how to awaken it. We define appraisals that awaken compassion as *generous interpretations* of suffering, meaning that they give people who are suffering the benefit of the doubt. These appraisals are grounded in what we refer to as a *positive default assumption*—a taken-for-granted stance that people who are suffering are good, capable, and worthy of compassion.

Learning to make more generous interpretations of suffering requires that we work to actively shift our assumptions. It also means that we must learn to look for the presence of suffering when we encounter failures, errors, declines in performance, missed deadlines, absences, delays in communication, or other difficult or ambiguous work events. Making generous interpretations inclines us to remember that these situations often mask suffering. More generous interpretations require that we suspend an immediate rush to judgment and instead draw on our curiosity about what might be causing circumstances where suffering hides.

WITHHOLDING BLAME

One way that we can make more generous interpretations of suffering is to withhold the assignment of blame when something has gone wrong or doesn't work out the way we think it should. The more we view someone as blameworthy, the less we can tap into empathy and concern. When we catch ourselves blaming someone for communicating poorly, missing a deadline, skipping a meeting, or dropping the ball on a task, we can draw on curiosity to ask about the causes and address the event directly. This does not mean letting a mistake slide or accommodating irresponsible behavior. It does mean kind and direct inquiry into what is happening whenever we don't understand someone's behavior. Just as inquiry work aids noticing, it also helps us to suspend judgment, withhold blame, and open space for interpreting with more generosity.

Our research shows that organizational messages maintaining a positive default assumption about people at work—that they are generally good, capable, and worthy of compassion—make these difficult dialogues about errors or unfortunate events easier. For instance, we studied organizational responses to Hurricane Sandy in New York. In some organizations, we found that leaders and managers would convey to members that employees who were absent or behind on work were good and capable but were suffering from the aftermath of the storm. These messages made it easier and more appropriate to interpret generously and cut some slack or give the benefit of the doubt. In contrast, in other organizations, leaders and managers would convey that the disaster was a chance for people to be lazy or take advantage of the system. Bulletins cautioned people against this kind of behavior, so it became harder to interpret generously. Instead, it seemed more appropriate to reinforce the rules and judge harshly if someone couldn't perform.

Making more generous interpretations of suffering may sound nice in theory, but in practice it represents what some teachers call *fierce compassion.*[7] It isn't easy to remain mindful and calm in the heat of the moment, when someone is acting out. It isn't easy to suspend judgment when someone is trying to put on a good face while making a mess at work. We will talk more about these difficult situations below. But withholding blame and engaging in compassionate conversations that allow generous interpretations about what's happening, while still setting high standards and holding people accountable for consequences, is one of the most skilled forms of workplace interaction we all must learn. These *crucial conversations* entail lifelong learning about how to hold true to work while making generous interpretations of suffering that generate solutions for both the person and the organization.[8]

IMBUING WITH WORTH

A second way that we can make more generous interpretations of suffering involves developing the ability to see others as worthy and deserving of compassion. Imbuing people with worth no matter their position in the organization, role, political stance, lifestyle, identity, economic status, or personality is no small feat. People who are different from us often seem undeserving of compassion in our eyes. As we said, these are blazing-fast stereotypical judgments that color our thinking automatically and implicitly. We can work to challenge them by actively practicing the positive default assumption and reminding ourselves of others' worth when we catch these judgments in our thinking.

We can make more generous interpretations by actively imbuing more people and their experiences with worth and dignity. For instance, middle managers aren't so often the target of our compassion. But they often suffer when they feel coerced to enforce rules or policies that cause distress. Because of their role and status, lower-level employees who suffer from a change enforced by the manager can forget the fact that the manager is suffering, too. And higher-level executives may not interpret the middle managers' suffering as worthy of compassion because they are just doing the job assigned to them. The difficult role has led some researchers to attend to the plight of middle managers, revealing their centrality in alleviating suffering for employees while suffering themselves during change.[9]

Interpretations of who is worthy of compassion are shaped by time demands at work, cultural differences across departments, status distinctions between headquarters and subsidiary units, and broader cultural stigmas. For example, in many cultures and organizations, mental health issues are not accepted as legitimate forms of suffering at work. The broader cultural stigma associated with depression, anxiety, and suicide silences mental health issues at work. In chapter 10, we will share a powerful leadership communication that serves to break the silence around suicide in an organization and offers a generous interpretation of this form of suffering and its organizational consequences. Rates of stress, anxiety, depression, burnout, and suicide are skyrocketing in professional settings. We can learn to make more generous interpretations of these widespread forms of human suffering, recognizing that the hyperconnected workplace has brought with it a plethora of challenges to our mental health. Giving others the benefit of the doubt that their stress, anxiety, and burnout is real and deserving of compassion will go a long way toward awakening compassion at work.

CULTIVATING PRESENCE

A third way in which we can learn to make more generous interpretations of suffering involves cultivating the belief that we have the capacity to meet suffering with compassion anytime it arises. When we feel we don't have the resources or skills to handle another's suffering, our sense that we can't handle it shuts down the process. But at times like these, when we think there's nothing we can "do," we can cultivate the ability to "be."[10] Philosopher Martin Buber made a similar point with his idea of the *I-Thou* relationship, noting the difference in our interactions when we shift from treating people as objects to recognizing the spark of the sacred or the infinite in the connection between ourselves and others.[11] Being present with another person who is suffering paves the way for compassion, even if we can't do anything to resolve the underlying causes of suffering. As we cultivate this capacity for presence in ourselves, we become more likely to interpret suffering generously. When we can be compassionate and keep our hearts open, we are less likely to fall prey to the interpretation that there's nothing we can do.[12]

These three forms of generous interpretation—withholding blame, imbuing with worth, and cultivating presence—are keys to whether or not we give people who are suffering the benefit of the doubt. When we make more generous interpretations of suffering, we expand our circle of concern and our capacity for compassionate action.

KEY POINTS: MAKING MORE GENEROUS INTERPRETATIONS OF SUFFERING

- ∞ Suffering is often masked by missed deadlines, errors, or difficult and ambiguous work situations that trigger blame instead of compassion.

- ∞ Learn to be curious about the causes of difficult or ambiguous work situations as a way of cultivating more generous interpretations.

- ∞ Practice a positive default assumption that others are good, capable, and worthy of compassion. Offer the benefit of the doubt.

- ∞ Withhold blame. Steer conversations about errors or failure toward learning.

- ∞ Imbue others with dignity and worth no matter their role, position, or difference from you.

∞ Cultivate presence with suffering as a form of being. Learning this skill helps you to avoid the interpretation that there is nothing you can do.

WHEN GENEROUS INTERPRETATIONS AREN'T EASY

Sociologist Kristen Monroe has dedicated a significant portion of her career to understanding the dynamics of people who risked their lives to rescue Jewish people from being persecuted during the Nazi takeover of Europe. Applying all the tools of social science, she attempted to find out what made a difference in the willingness and desire to save someone from death or torture. Was it race, class, gender, education, family size, nationality, profession, religion, or even whether one was a rural person or urban dweller? In the end, none of those explained why someone would risk life and home for the sake of another. Instead, what mattered most was a mind-set toward shared humanity. Irene, a holocaust rescuer in Poland, explained succinctly the motivation that all these rescuers shared: "We all belong to one human family."[13]

Many life experiences could foster this belief. Experiences of work are one. Workplaces offer the opportunity to be in community with others and experience being part of an interconnected whole. When we tap into this sense of shared human family at work, workplaces have tremendous power to bring out compassion that otherwise lies dormant and untapped. In this book, we will often refer to the positive default assumption that people are good and worthy of compassion as our shared humanity. What we mean by shared humanity is captured in Kristin Monroe's description as well: "I would characterize it as a different way of seeing things; it certainly represents a different way of seeing the world and one-self in relation to others. . . . A particular perspective in which all mankind is connected through a common humanity, in which each individual is linked to all others and to a world in which all living beings are entitled to a certain human treatment by virtue of be-ing alive."[14] While we know that organizations can foster this view, certainly it is also easy to lose sight of our shared humanity when social barriers begin to divide us.

WHEN WE AREN'T IN IT TOGETHER

For as much as work can remind us that we all belong to one human family, it can undermine that sense equally powerfully. There are times when we aren't all in it together. Our aspirations are put to the test when we encounter people who aren't doing their work or are taking advantage of the compassion of others. In fact, many people worry about being taken advantage of if they are compassionate at work. Awakening compassion at work means confronting this worry directly.

Elsie told a story about being a long-time employee in a maga-zine publishing firm. She knew how to manage her deadlines, so on a day when she needed to make some phone calls about cancer care for her father, she took time out of work to talk to the hospital, knowing that it would not impact her schedule. Marla, a relatively new coworker sitting in a nearby cubicle, left a stack of additional articles that needed editing on Elsie's chair over her lunch hour. On the top of the stack of paper, Marla left a note that read: "These are for you, since you don't have anything else to do." Elsie felt shocked and hurt by the note. When she tried to talk to Marla, however, Marla reacted angrily and shouted at Elsie about her lack of a work ethic. Elsie sought the intervention of a manager. The manager glossed over Marla's uncivil behavior by telling Elsie, "You know, Marla's under a lot of stress right now." While at times this suggestion could have fed into a generous interpretation for Marla's behavior that might have resonated with Elsie, in this instance the manager's words sounded hollow and insincere. Elsie felt the manager was making an excuse for Marla in a desire to escape dealing with the situation in a more direct manner.

Making more generous interpretations of suffering does involve looking for hidden causes of workplace behaviors like Marla's incivility. That does not mean that we are stripped of responsibility for managing them well, however. In fact, awakening compassion at work requires the opposite. What many managers and leaders do not recognize is that compassion at work is not soft and fuzzy. Said dramatically by Margot, another holocaust rescuer in Kristin Monroe's research: "You don't walk away. You don't walk away from somebody who needs real help—even if this is someone who 'is terrible.'"[15] In less dramatic terms, compassion at work requires not turning away from people who seem to be difficult to deal with, feckless, incompetent, lazy, or emotionally unaware. Our shared humanity requires that we manage these situations in ways that do not allow them to perpetuate suffering at work.

WHEN WE HAVE TO LET GO

While some supervisors allow a poorly performing employee to flame out and leave rather than addressing the issue directly, awakening compassion at work requires that we make more generous interpretations of suffering even when we have to let people go. Leaders, managers, and employees who have to let people go during restructuring or downsizing sometimes hide behind legal concerns rather than having compassionate conversations that explain the decision. This comes at a cost to both the employees and the organization. Recall the research we cited in chapter 2 showing that compassionate downsizing practices yield financial resilience.

In our research we encountered a manager, Terrell, who awakened compassion even as he had to let an employee go for performance reasons. When William didn't show up for work one day and didn't call in sick, Terrell knew that something was amiss. William had never done that in over ten years of being an employee. Terrell called William and left a message, but the call went unreturned. At the end of the day, Terrell called again and left a message expressing concern. It wasn't until the next morning that William's wife phoned. Timidly, she explained that William hadn't reported for work because he had been arrested. A drug addiction that William had kept a secret from his coworkers and manager, even from his wife and kids, had finally overtaken his ability to hide it. Terrell felt shocked and betrayed. As a small business owner who had been dedicated to his employees over a long time, he was hurt and angry that William had lied to him and missed the opportunity to seek help and support before it was too late. While he helped William's wife handle the legal procedures to get him out of jail, Terrell found himself wondering about what to do. What was the nature of a truly compassionate response?

Terrell informed other employees that William would be taking several days off. Without explaining or conveying judgment about William, he simply helped people to coordinate in William's absence. Terrell took time to think. After a few days, when he felt that he could talk with William without overreacting, he met with William privately and conveyed his hurt and disappointment. He listened to William's story of what had happened. Terrell listened with empathy and suggested that William could no longer work under the influence of drugs. Terrell suggested that he pour all his energy into drug treatment. Terrell allowed William to announce his departure, and William was able to leave with dignity. Terrell found that true compassion in this case involved both a generous interpretation of William's ability to recover, and being willing and able to let William go.

Another type of compassionate letting go involves conflicts at work. Colleagues in conflict with one another often slip into uncivil interactions, taking revenge on each other as Marla did to Elsie. Other times, conflict breeds cold silences that hinder collaboration. These conflicts require working things through and letting go of grudges. We can awaken compassion at work through more generous interpretations of suffering that comes from these conflicts, as well as developing greater skill in addressing them with compassion.[16] But many managers and leaders overlook this interpersonal corrosiveness, thinking that there is little they can do about it. As we saw above, cultivating the capacity to be compassionate even when we cannot solve the underlying problem is a powerful key to compassion. We witnessed this in our research, with Sarah, the leader of Midwest Billing, a group we will describe more in chapter 9. Sarah engaged extensively in helping people let go of conflicts at work. She was challenged to maintain her generous interpretations of suffering when an employee verbally attacked her in front of the whole group. Sarah described this as one of her most difficult moments as a manager: "I can tell you something that happened that is the personal thing I am probably most proud of as a leader, because it could have been really messy." Her unit had just taken over a large new project, and tension was high. Jada volunteered to lead the project group. Sarah explained, "A couple of the people that we hired didn't end up fitting into the group like we thought they would. The stress level was going up, and we tried something that didn't work. Everyone felt even worse after the failure. Jada needed to vent."

Sarah was known for keeping her door open to people who wanted to talk about work stress. This time, however, Jada did not visit Sarah's office privately. "For some reason, Jada decided to vent at our daily morning meeting, and she lost control. She wasn't just letting me know her dissatisfaction with what was going on, but she got into yelling, crying, name calling, and it became a kind of a personal attack on me. And I just stood there. I knew that to try to rebut anything, or to refute anything, or to get into this argument was going to be a losing battle. So I let it go all the way through. It went on maybe twenty minutes, a very intense twenty minutes. Most of the members of the unit were in tears just hearing it. Then Jada got up and left. She ran out, grabbed her purse, and left. I told everyone that the meeting was adjourned, and I went to my office to regroup."

Sarah felt outraged. She knew that she could fire Jada for this outburst. She did not know if Jada would even return to work after running out of the meeting. But a few hours later, Jada returned. "I was in the kitchen; a bunch of people were also in the kitchen. She walked in and said, 'I am so sorry.' This was a very sincere, from-her-heart apology. She said, 'I lost it. I lost it. And I wouldn't blame you a bit if you fired me.' Right then, I made a choice. I went and I put my arms around her and I said, 'I forgive you.'" As a manager with a lot of experience, Sarah had a sense that there was something else happening for Jada. "I asked her, 'Do you want to come into my office and talk?' And that's when everything started coming out. She'd found out a couple days before that her husband was having an affair. Jada has four children. I let her go through it all, and then I just put my arms back around her and I said, 'Jada, I forgive you.'"

So we see again that compassion isn't always gentle and warm—it's a different form of managerial toughness.[17] "I'm proud of that,"

Sarah concluded. "One of the things that makes me proud isn't just the fact that I felt that something else was going on, but the fact that she came to the realization that she was wrong. And that she could come back and feel comfortable enough to come in and apologize and make things right, even if she was going to be fired."

Sometimes compassion requires the courage to speak honestly about what is unacceptable. Sometimes it means standing up to disrespect and incivility and intervening to stop people from manipulating the system.[18] Sometimes it involves forgiving and forgoing our desire for vengeance or punishment.[19] On some occasions, with some people, claims of suffering may not be truthfully represented. In such cases, further exploration of a person's circumstances may call up feelings of being taken advantage of or misled. The process of interpreting suffering is consequential. For compassion to flow, generous interpretations must be accompanied by a belief that a person's pain is real.

KEY POINTS: WHEN GENEROUS INTERPRETATIONS AREN'T EASY

- ∞ Work can remind us that we all belong to one human family and emphasize our shared humanity, supporting generous interpretations of one another's suffering.

- ∞ Generous interpretations of suffering are challenging when we encounter poor performance, broken trust, manipulation, disrespect, or other uncivil behaviors at work, but these challenges call for compassionate action.

- ∞ Fierce compassion involves refusing to perpetuate suffering in work situations, which can involve letting people go or standing up to disrespectful behavior.

- ∞ Generous interpretations of suffering help to keep us from acting out of vengeance or punishing others when suffering erupts in inappropriate ways at work.

■ AN INVITATION TO REFLECT ON GENEROUS INTERPRETATIONS OF SUFFERING

A simple question like "Is everything OK?" may open a tender conversation where we must learn to proceed without judgment or blame, simply listening with a sense of shared humanity. Setting aside for a moment the need to fix or solve or do, we focus simply on being present with suffering and doing the inward work of making more generous interpretations of the human being who needs a listening ear. Even when there is nothing else we can do, imbuing someone with worth and dignity moves us toward compassion.

When work organizations drive out suffering by wrapping pain with harsh judgments, people who can make generous interpretations allow compassion back in. These appraisals of suffering—how we explain the suffering and its causes to ourselves and others—are key to responding with compassion. How we lean into the meaning of suffering at work can either break our workplaces open with empathy or seal them up with disdain. Compassion writers Daniel Homan and Lonni Collins Pratt emphasize the importance of such generous interpretations when they observe, "When I reach past my own ideas, I begin to stretch myself open to the world, and this opening of my heart could change everything."[20]

Have you had an experience when your heart opened and you had to stretch beyond the you/me divide to call upon your membership in the broader human family? Recognizing that these interpretations are the key to responding, what does this moment reveal about awakening compassion in your work?

5

FEELING:
THE BRIDGE TO
COMPASSIONATE
ACTION

IN HER EXPLORATION OF how we live out the concept of empathy, writer Leslie Jamison makes the point that empathy is both a feeling and a choice: "Empathy isn't just something that happens to us—a meteor shower of synapses firing across the brain—it's also a choice we make: to pay attention, to extend ourselves. It's made of exertion, that dowdier cousin of impulse."[1] Contemporary scientific research echoes Jamison's observations, with neuroscience and laboratory studies validating the fact that empathy is both a largely automatic feeling and an effort that is under the control of our choices.[2] This research shows that while empathy can happen instantly, it doesn't always. People can take on other people's postures, facial expressions, and feelings after just a fraction of a second of being together, and this automatic social connection is undergirded by mirrored or synchronous patterns of brain activity.[3] But sometimes we close our hearts and minds instead.

We have the capacity to "turn on" and "turn off" feelings of concern for other people. Research shows that this capacity is strongly influenced by perceptions of empathy's social benefits and costs, such as how much time or effort we think it will take to empathize with someone or how emotionally taxing it seems, given what's going on in the situation.[4] Researcher Jamil Zaki suggests that the fact that we can choose empathy is hopeful because it shows that we can grow our empathy in two ways, each of which is important for awakening compassion at work.[5] First, we can build individual skills that help us to understand our own and other people's emotional lives and connect in deeper ways. We will talk about some of those skills in this chapter. Second, we can create organizations that make empathy more desirable and rewarding, which science shows is a reliable way to increase people's feelings of concern. We will explore that more in the third section of the book, when we talk about how to design systems that amplify compassion.

A GLANCE AT THE SCIENCE OF EMPATHY

By looking at empathy more closely, scientists now emphasize that this word encompasses multiple human processes of relating, including knowing another person's feelings and thoughts, feeling what another person feels, imagining oneself in another person's circumstances, feeling concern for another person's suffering, and more.[6] The science of empathy is complex and changing rapidly, so we will just take a glance at this fascinating field and what it tells us about awakening compassion at work.

Unlike theories of the past that suggested a drive for self-interest was primary or exclusive in human nature, the new science of compassion and neuroscientific investigations of empathy are leading us to understand that the capacity for empathy and human connection is innately core to human nature.[7] New studies show that we can pick up on suffering and respond with concern based on even the slightest facial expressions or voice cues. Brain imaging allows us to see in new ways that when we are confronted with the pain of social exclusion, it shows up in our brains, and our bodies respond to it as physical pain.[8] And when we see someone else in pain, we sometimes actually experience it as physical pain ourselves.[9]

In relation to compassion at work, we focus on two ways in which we come to feel empathy. The first is cognitive, referring to our ability to stand in someone else's shoes—in research this is called *perspective taking*. The second is emotional, referring to our ability to feel concern for what others are going through—called *empathic concern*. Throughout the book, we will refer to empathy as the feeling part of the compassion process, and we will highlight how feeling concern for others motivates compassionate action. This does not negate the fact that to feel empathy is also a cognitive choice—in fact, we hope that our work reveals both new ways to increase feelings of empathy and new reasons to choose it.

Empathy can be difficult to access at work. Our willingness and capacity to feel concern for other people or take their perspective is easily blocked by task focus, time pressure, and the high cost of making errors.[10] When work conditions make empathy seem costly—for instance, if expressing concern for someone who made a mistake might make us seem equally to blame—we might shut down our feelings.[11] We may actually feel indifference or even aversion when we encounter suffering at work if the situation is costly. So while our brains are wired with the capacity to feel empathy instantly and automatically in the presence of others, our work may put obstacles in our path.[12] When that happens, we have to choose to extend ourselves, to take others' perspectives, and to invite the feelings that widen our circles of concern.

SKILLS THAT FOSTER
EMPATHIC CONCERN

Our glance at the science shows that we can increase empathy by building skills that make us more capable of connecting with others. These skills help us choose empathy when we need it. Let's look at this somewhat abstract point from research as it might appear in a workplace. We found an instance that shows both how feelings of empathy can be blocked by factors in the work context and how skill can restore empathic concern and motivate compassionate action.

Juana wanted someday to become a paralegal in a law firm. As a copy clerk, she would pick up documents from the desks of the paralegals and receive her instructions on how many times to duplicate them, thinking about what it would be like to work at such a big desk. She just had a locker in the basement. When a partner in the firm marked up a paper and put a sticky note on top asking for a book, Juana would gladly visit the library. She would look at the books with interest and deliver the parcel to the large offices on the upper floors of the building, imagining how it would feel to know everything in those books. But most days didn't offer much reality where Juana's dream of further study or advancement could take root. She ran errands, copied and stamped, mailed and printed and labeled. Often, while she worked, the steady rhythm of pages feeding into the machines felt like background music to her worry about whether her ex-husband was going pay his child support, how she could afford more training, or how she was going to feed the kids. When the drumbeat of worry grew loud, Juana caught herself making mistakes.

Juana's mistakes irritated Rosita, a paralegal who depended on Juana for help. Rosita knew that Juana was usually reliable, but she grew impatient when she asked for five copies and only four arrived, or when she had to ask Juana to correct the filing dates stamped in big red letters on the legal documents. The staff manager on their floor, Veronica, happened to walk by Rosita's desk and heard her say harshly to Juana, "You only made four copies of this SEC filing, but I asked you for five. How many times do I have to ask you before you get it right?"

Veronica was worried that work pressures were stamping out Rosita's capacity to feel empathy for Juana. Veronica knew that Rosita was a stickler for perfection, but she was also usually supportive of other women in the office and was one of the most talented paralegals in the fast-track program that Veronica had created for assistants who wanted to move up in the organization. Veronica also knew that Juana was great at her job. She hoped that Juana, too, would benefit from the fast-track program over time, but Juana would need Rosita's recommendation to get into the program. Feeling concerned for both Juana and Rosita, Veronica decided to intervene in this dynamic.

Organizational scholar John Shotter describes how people like Veronica draw upon feelings of empathic concern to act in the face of the unknown regularly at work, doing what he calls "feeling our way forward."[13] As we'll see below, that's what Veronica did. She invited Rosita and Juana to make an empathic choice to work together differently. Their story, which comes from our research, illustrates four skills that support feeling our way forward together.

PERCEPTIVE ENGAGEMENT

The first set of skills that support feeling our way forward together hinges on making the distinction between the cognitive and emotional dimensions of empathy. Cognitive aspects of empathy help us see another's point of view or imagine ourselves in someone else's situation, which also helps us feel concern for the person.

Compassion teacher Karla McLaren calls the skill set of exercising cognitive empathy *perceptive engagement*, by which she means not only taking the other's perspective, but also using this perspective to discern what will be helpful for someone who may be very different from us.[14]

Perceptive engagement helped Veronica to address the conflict between Rosita and Juana. She began by asking Rosita to stop by her office for a minute. Once Rosita sat down, Veronica dug in to unpack both Rosita's and Juana's perspectives. "I wanted to ask you about Juana's work. I overhead you correcting an error today, and I've noticed that her work seems a bit off this week. I know this is frustrating. But I also know that you value supporting your coworkers. You and Juana usually work together well. I wonder, do you know whether something else is behind this pattern?" Notice the quality of Veronica's inquiry work, gently drawing attention to the possibility of suffering and inviting a more generous interpretation. Veronica continued, "Of course, we can't afford a continual stream of mistakes. But I don't think everything's quite right. So I wanted your perspective." Veronica's skill in taking Rosita's perspective opened space for an authentic conversation. It also invited Rosita to take Juana's perspective into account. By deepening their collective perceptive engagement, Veronica made it more likely that they could find a solution to support high-quality work simultaneously with compassion both for Rosita's frustration and for Juana's life circumstances.

ATTUNEMENT

Another skill that is essential for opening up space to feel more empathic concern is often referred to as *attunement*. In research terms, attunement involves being aware of another person while simultaneously directing attention toward our own bodily somatic senses and discerning how we are interconnected with each other. In the words of compassion teacher Joan Halifax: "You open a space in which the encounter can unfold, in which you are present for whatever may arise, in yourself and in [another]."[15] Deeply skilled attunement is often a part of the training involved for performing therapeutic or healing work. In some workplaces, such as hospice, nursing, and social service, attunement is a valued clinical skill.[16] In other workplaces, it is more of an invisible but crucial aspect of working together well. Attunement is equally valuable on a hospital ward, a manufacturing floor, and a meeting room. Managers with a capacity for attunement perform better in the eyes of their subordinates, and colleagues who practice attunement work together more seamlessly and engage in higher quality collaboration.

Veronica's questions heightened Rosita's capacity for attunement. After her conversation with Veronica, Rosita stopped by the copy room to see Juana. Rosita didn't know it, but Juana's worries about her life outside of work were nearly overwhelming her. There was just enough gas in her car to get home that night, but not enough to get all the way back tomorrow. There was no formula in the refrigerator for the baby. The kids would be hungry for dinner and attention. Her former husband hadn't stopped by with the check he had promised. Feeling hot tears rising, Juana held them back. She didn't want anyone at work to see her cry.

When Rosita tapped her on the shoulder, Juana was so anxious that she literally jumped. Rosita began to apologize for losing her temper, which took Juana by surprise. The tears that had been on the edge of her eyelids all afternoon rose into her eyes again. "It's OK. You were right. I made a mistake." Juana turned a little, as if to go.

But Rosita was attuned to Juana's suffering now. She asked Juana to wait. Reiterating that the mistake wasn't Juana's usual work pattern, she asked a gentle question that would open up space for the possibility of a more generous interpretation of Juana's errors at work as well as more empathy: "Wait. This isn't like you, and I'm sorry I snapped before. Why don't you tell me, is something else going on?"

EMPATHIC LISTENING

A third skill that is essential in the workplace and fundamental for awakening compassion is what scholars call empathic listening. Empathic listening requires us to be tuned in enough to deeply hear another person's perspective and to listen for the emotion behind the words. Empathic listening can be difficult when we think that it will be hard to hear someone's suffering. It is also difficult to listen this way when we feel there is nothing we can "do" to fix the situation, because we will tend to shut down our empathy in the face of these costs. But research shows that we can choose to tap into our feelings of concern rather than close them down. When we do so, cultivating presence and validating the other person's experience, our empathy makes a difference even if we cannot change the circumstances.[17]

For Rosita, as she became attuned to Juana's worry, she also deepened her listening and was able to approach Juana's story with a feeling of concern. Her frustration with Juana melted into the background as she listened to the description of her worries about affording gas and groceries and the difficulty of relying on her ex-husband for financial support for her children. Rosita remained attentive, watching Juana closely but kindly, hearing the anxiety and fear behind the words. Rosita did not interrupt or try to make suggestions. She simply sat with Juana and listened. Once Juana had finished her story, Rosita expressed her concern for Juana and acknowledged the stress of this kind of worry. She acknowledged the challenges Juana was facing and how difficult they felt, and she relayed a story from her own life that put Juana at ease. This helped restore their working relationship and boosted their willingness to cooperate and get things done quickly and efficiently.

MINDFUL ATTENTION

A fourth skill that helps us to develop more empathic concern for each other at work involves what scholars refer to as *mindfulness*— defined as an embodied awareness of what is happening in ourselves, in others, and in our environment on a moment-to-moment basis.[18] This skillful way of being present counterbalances the pressures and distractions of work environments that can get in the way of our feelings of concern. Techniques for developing mindfulness range from focusing our thoughts as we take a deep breath to repeating a word or phrase or visualizing our bodies in some form of systemic relaxation. Scientists studying people who engage in such practices have documented their beneficial effects, such as better sleep, improvements in health, a reduction in stress, the cultivation of a calm demeanor, better regulation of emotion, and a heightened capacity to remain present with others.[19]

At work, mindfulness helps us to be better prepared to remain calm and present when we encounter suffering. For instance, Veronica was able to be mindful in the midst of Rosita's anger and engage in a conversation that deepened Rosita's empathy. Rosita was also able to remain mindful of what was happening for both herself and for Juana as she listened to Juana's story. Her mindful attention and her ability to remain calm fueled her feelings of concern. Later that day, as Rosita reflected on her conversation with Juana, her mind flashed to the pride of her own mother, who'd worked two jobs to feed her children and support their education. When she had chastised Juana for making a mistake, Rosita had no idea that she was adding a straw to an almost-broken back. Mindfulness helped Rosita to shift her perspective of Juana from someone who was making a lot of mistakes and needed criticizing to someone with dignity who needed support to get through a really tough situation.

As she reflected, Rosita felt moved to do something else. Leaving work a little early, she walked to the little market across the street. She purchased a bag of groceries, grabbing milk, bread, cereal, and fruit. It was enough for breakfast, at least. She took the bag back to the office building and placed it squarely in front of Juana's locker, so that she would find it before she left. Rosita also tucked a plain white envelope into Juana's locker door, safe but in sight, containing enough money to buy some gas for the next day.

When she got to her locker, Juana found the food bag and envelope. Slipping her finger under the flap, she glimpsed the edge of a $20 bill. There was no note. Juana turned the envelope over in her hands as if it were a miracle. She knew it must have been Rosita who had left this for her. Rosita's understanding and expression of genuine concern made this seem like a gift rather than demeaning pity, which Juana didn't want. Juana vowed to work even harder to demonstrate that she deserved Rosita's compassion. Veronica's skilled perceptive engagement had paved the way for Rosita's empathy to blossom into compassionate action at work—compassionate action that heightened work engagement and commitment in invisible but powerful ways.

While the details of their story are unique, Veronica, Rosita, and Juana could be any of us. When we dedicate ourselves to practicing these four skill sets, we too pave the way for workplaces that are filled with empathy and compassion.

KEY POINTS: SKILLS THAT SUPPORT EMPATHY AT WORK

∞ Build skill in perceptive engagement, the capacity to take another person's perspective and discern what would be helpful.

∞ Cultivate capacity for attunement, which involves being aware of another person while simultaneously staying in touch with our own somatic senses and experiences. It heightens our sense of interconnection.

∞ Develop empathic listening, the capacity to tune in to feelings of concern as we hear another person's perspectives and experiences. It allows us to be present without needing to fix, solve, or intervene.

∞ Foster mindfulness, an awareness of changing conditions in ourselves and others on a moment-to-moment basis. It helps us to remain calm and steady in the face of suffering—our own as well as that of others.

∞ Empathy at work helps us to "feel our way forward" together and motivates compassion.

IDENTIFICATION AND EMPATHY AT WORK

In his book *The Age of Empathy*, primatologist Frans de Waal writes, "Empathy's chief portal is identification. We're ready to share the feelings of someone we identify with, which is why we do so easily with those who belong to our inner circle."[20] Identification with others at work is an important way that we can broaden our circle of concern and awaken compassion. This identification can come about through a sense that we have had similar experiences, even if we are different from one another in many other ways. We can identify with colleagues by sensing that we are at similar career stages, we are learning similar skills, we are engaged in similar kinds of work, or we have similar interests. Through these forms of identification, workplaces can spark empathic concern and compassion among people who might otherwise never open up to one another.

We can see the power of subtle forms of identification in laboratory research on empathy. Social psychologists Piercarlo Valdesolo and David DeSteno invented a creative experimental way to show that if we feel similar to one another, even in subconscious ways, we are more likely to act with compassion.[21] They paired partners who sat opposite one another at a table, each looking at a computer monitor. The participants had to tap on a sensor as they listened to tunes playing in their headphones. As part of the study, in some pairs one partner tapped out of time with the other partner while in other pairs the partners tapped on the same beat. After the computer task, partners filled out a questionnaire. The results showed that those who had tapped in synchrony felt more similar to each other and were more willing to help each other on a later task.

These kinds of effects extend beyond the laboratory as well. In our research we met Ken, an accomplished entrepreneur who had built several successful ventures. Ken had joined an investing group after the success of his last start-up, partly to see a range of new ideas and partly to encourage younger entrepreneurs. It was in this context that he met Daniel, who was also an accomplished entrepreneur and an experienced investor who coached new entrepreneurs. Though they didn't know each other well, Ken and Daniel shared some interesting conversations at these angel investing group meetings. Ken was impressed with Daniel's knowledge. Daniel came across as a bit gruff and mostly kept to himself, but this wasn't unusual for an investor of his stature.

"Then one day Daniel showed up at my house distraught and at loose ends," Ken recalled. "He was sobbing and incoherent, so I stayed with him." Ken, untrained in psychology and unsure of what to do, drew upon a deep sense of empathic concern for Daniel to feel his way forward and get help. "Eventually I took him to hospital for a kind of urgent clinical care." Ken did not know why Daniel turned to him, but perhaps the identification that was born from their shared backgrounds and work experiences acted in the same way that the laboratory tapping task had for strangers—bringing them together in an invisible web of similarity that fostered empathy. Daniel's bouts with depression and seeking out Ken's help became an enduring pattern. As Ken described it, "For three years or so he was not so good. . . . But for some reason he glommed onto me. And every once in a while, every month or so, I'd get a call and I would have to go wherever he was and be with him."

We don't know why Daniel sensed that he could turn to Ken in a deep time of need. Something in their work identification created trust that Ken would come to his aid. Ken helped Daniel get the professional mental health care he needed. Ken and Daniel's story is a powerful illustration of how identification in work fuels empathy and compassion that may extend far beyond work as well. Summoned arbitrarily by a colleague in distress, some of us might not put our life on hold and go to be with the person on a regular basis. In this work relationship, however, a seed of similarity ripened into a blossom of empathic concern that helped Ken and Daniel find their way forward together with compassion.

CULTIVATING IDENTIFICATION THROUGH PRESENCE

Cultivating identification with others at work in ways that will fuel empathy and compassion requires being available, both physically and psychologically. Availability becomes real in organizations through simple gestures such as keeping one's door open, arriving early for a meeting, holding online office hours for distributed teams, or lingering in a kitchen or a break room to be around others. Any of these small acts to make ourselves accessible opens the space for connection and mutual engagement that is a powerful form of care.[22] Another participant in our research, Ralph, a professor and former dean, gave us a powerful example of the impact of this form of availability: "My wife and I lost three close relatives in one year—my mother and father, and her brother, who died of a heart attack at thirty-seven years of age. A lot of people came to our door and chatted about relatives that had died, and so on, but one couple came to our door and wept. And I said, 'Well, come on in.' So, they came in. They didn't say anything. . . . And it's interesting, because at the end of the day, my wife and I would go over the day's grieving. And the couple that really served us and cared for us and showed compassion was the couple that had said nothing, but had listened and hugged and wept with us."[23]

Leaders who convey psychological presence with others in the organization are often described as great leaders who can command loyalty and commitment. And in the hyperconnected technological world of work, physical and psychological presence becomes a deeply meaningful gesture. Turning off the cell phone to be with someone is a move toward identification and empathy. Opening the door to another person's experience and shutting off the email is another. When we need to bear witness to someone else's suffering, as Ken did with Daniel, presence helps us to identify and tune in to feeling empathic concern. So, to identify at work is often to sit down, close the door to distractions, turn off the ringer, and open the door to our hearts.

Scholar Edward Hallowell writes about this kind of presence as "the human moment at work." He insists that creating these human moments requires us to defy the daily grind: "You have to set aside what you are doing, put down the memo you were reading, disengage from your laptop, abandon your daydream, and focus on the person you are with."[24] These forms of presence are important in fueling identification. The science of compassion shows us that if we are physically present but psychologically absent, we telegraph our lack of interest and disengagement through posture, body language, lack of eye contact, and a failure to ask questions. All of these signals close the door to identification with one another and to feeling empathic concern that motivates compassionate action.

KEY POINTS: IDENTIFICATION FOSTERS EMPATHY

∞ When we identify with others, we are more likely to feel empathy for them and more willing to take compassionate action on their behalf.

∞ Feeling similar to someone, even in subtle ways, contributes to identification.

∞ Physical and psychological presence, conveyed through eye contact, verbal tone, posture, and facial expressions, heighten identification.

∞ Human moments at work, when we set aside distractions and focus on people who are in pain, heighten our ability to identify with one another and awaken compassion.

AN INVITATION TO REFLECT ON EMPATHY AS A BRIDGE TO ACTION

Hidden under organizational charts and strategic plans, empathic concern is a feeling that connects us at work. Research shows us that this feeling is a powerful motivator for compassionate action. Sensitive to costs, empathy can be fragile, but we can choose to extend ourselves to another regardless. While organizations can dampen empathic concern in many ways, they can also heighten it by helping us identify with others who are similar in some way. When we feel more similar to others through workplace connections, empathy grows. We can learn and practice skills of perceptive engagement, attunement, mindfulness, and empathic listening to grow empathy even further. As a bridge to compassionate action, this powerful feeling instantaneously invites us to feel our way forward together.

When has a connection with someone at work suddenly flowered with empathy and concern in ways that moved you toward compassion? Recognizing this as the bridge to action, what does this moment reveal about awakening compassion in your work?

ACTING: THE MOVES THAT ALLEVIATE SUFFERING AT WORK

IN THE WORLD OF WORK, compassion is expressed in action. Our research has uncovered the fact that compassion at work is largely improvisational, meaning that actions often have to be made up on the spot, shaped in ways that correspond with the unique circumstances of suffering. Like improv actors who make up their lines as they go or jazz musicians who build off of one another's notes, compassionate actions are creative moves that build off of interpretations of suffering, feelings of empathic concern, and perceptive engagement about what will be helpful. Unlike actors or musicians, however, most managers and leaders don't receive training or know how to deliberately build skill in acting with compassion. We can remedy this lack of training and preparation. Research demonstrates that managing with compassion is learnable and can be developed through practice.[1]

When actions taken to alleviate suffering are improvisational, creative, and skillfully devised to meet unique, idiosyncratic needs,

we refer to them as compassion *moves*. Moves are more than acts—
they represent skillful and practical knowing-in-action. Workplace
compassion moves that are based in our knowledge about someone
else help in two ways: they alleviate suffering and they keep work going. Compassion moves fit both the needs of people and the norms
and routines that govern work life.

COMMON COMPASSION MOVES

Our research uncovered examples of many common and important
compassion moves at work. Nazima's story, adapted from our research,
illustrates many. Nazima got a phone call from her sister Chenni in
the middle of a workday, and she knew instantly that something must
be wrong. Chenni's voice reinforced Nazima's instinctive feeling of
concern. "There's been an accident," Chenni said. "Faith has died."
Nazima and Chenni shared a special bond that had been strengthened
when Chenni's daughter, Faith, had been born with Down syndrome.
Nazima had spent a lot of time with the family and was close to Faith.
Nazima had grown closer to her sister as her relationship with her
niece evolved. Chenni relayed a story of a terrible and tragic accident
that had taken Faith's life that day. Nazima listened, stunned.

Nazima occupied an important role in her organization, running crucial projects. When Chenni called, she had been preparing
for the largest board meeting of the year, involving a complex budget
review and discussion of other sensitive issues. She was due to get
on a plane later that afternoon to travel to the meeting. She felt immediately that she could not go, though she knew it was going to
place a heavy burden on others to cover for her. Nazima called Ed,
a colleague who was also due to travel and attend the meeting. Ed's
response was instant: "Your sister needs you. Don't worry about the
meeting. I'll handle everything."

FLEXIBLE TIME TO COPE WITH SUFFERING

Ed recalled that conversation with Nazima vividly. "There was no question in my mind about the priorities for Nazima or our team," he said. "I would step in and do whatever was necessary. She absolutely needed to be able to choose to be with her family." At times like this, providing people with flexibility is an important compassion move. Some people cope with suffering by being completely present with their families or loved ones and bowing out of work in the midst of grief and loss. Others prefer to work. Still others wish to remain partially involved in work. Accommodating unique preferences with flexible time arrangements is an important aspect of making this compassion move work.

While we might think that this is an easy or obvious compassion move, in reality not all organizations or work relationships support it. LaShonda, a woman we interviewed, recalled a time when her mother-in-law died and she asked her longtime supervisor for time off. The supervisor responded by telling LaShonda that he didn't handle schedule requests: "I have staff who handle this, and I don't want to deal with it." Ultimately, LaShonda was not granted time off. She described the suffering that this lack of flexibility caused for her and her family, exacerbating the grief that they already felt: "I do remember it as a very uncompassionate moment. I reported to work and missed the viewing at the funeral home. My husband was very upset I couldn't be there. We had four family members staying with us, but I was expected to be at work, so my husband had to handle things at home with the guests, plus arrange the service at our church and attend a church meal alone. I missed spending that day with twenty-eight members of our family there and missed out on a lot." Flexible time to cope can be difficult to come by in an organizational topography of deadlines, pressures to perform, and routines that won't wait. But suffering doesn't conform to any organizational timetable. Improvisational compassion moves must accommodate the need to get things done as well as to care for those who are suffering, as Ed did when he picked up Nazima's work and freed her to attend to her sister.

TASK FLEXIBILITY AND BUFFERING

Another set of compassion moves can be described as creating task flexibility that buffers the person in need from a deluge of communication. This compassion move involves creating choices for people who are suffering to engage with work tasks in varying ways depending on their preferences and abilities. It can also involve filtering information and questions through someone who acts as a buffer, protecting the suffering person from being overwhelmed. In Nazima's case, for instance, Ed checked in with others in the organization, informing them of Faith's death and suggesting that they work with him for anything involving Nazima. Ed became a buffer for task-related questions and issues, freeing Nazima to focus on her family while he kept things going at work. Others in the organization did not need to try to coordinate with Nazima, since they could redirect their questions to Ed to keep work moving. Sometimes buffering is invisible to those we are protecting, so inquiring about people's preferences for work communication helps calibrate these compassion moves. Ed buffered Nazima from work requests in a skillful, sensitive manner, checking in with her regularly. As a buffer, Ed also became a conduit of expressions of sympathy from other coworkers, which comforted Nazima but didn't overwhelm her.

MONITORING AND LISTENING

Because circumstances can change quickly in times of suffering, a third type of compassion move involves monitoring or regularly checking in on someone's condition. Once again, this compassion move can be improvised to fit the needs and preferences of the people involved, but a quick check-in that works for people who are suffering helps ensure that even while they have freedom from work tasks, they know that they are not alone. The information from regular monitoring and listening to someone who is suffering also helps bolster feelings of concern and provides information to help people customize and sustain compassionate actions. In Nazima's case, Ed checked in daily in small ways, such as email or text message, just to let Nazima know that he was thinking of her. Once every few days, or when Nazima requested to talk, Ed phoned her. He reiterated that she didn't need to worry about things at work. The consistent monitoring allowed Nazima to take advantage of Ed's feelings of concern and his skilled empathic listening. Nazima expressed worries for her sister, feeling comforted by Ed's acknowledgment of the challenges. While there was nothing more tangible that Ed could do, his being compassionate and listening comforted Nazima.

REASSURANCE AND SAFETY

Ed consistently reassured Nazima that she did not need to worry about work and that her job was safe. This is a fourth type of compassion move: offering reassurance and safety. When people are suffering, knowing that their job is safe relieves a heavy burden of worry. Significant forms of suffering can entail extended absences. When people are offered generous interpretations of their absence, this reassurance becomes a form of compassion. Ed's organization offered Nazima all the time she needed to be with her sister. Nazima knew from Ed's reassurance, as well as from his sustained attention and his expressions of concern, that he and others were engaging in generous interpretations of her absence. She felt more able to be compassionate with her family because of the compassion she was receiving from Ed and her colleagues. Again, while this may seem like an obvious compassion move, not all organizations offer reassurances of job security or safety in the face of unexpected or protracted suffering. Many bereavement-leave policies offer only a few days of excused absence. Other jobs offer no sick leave or personal leave of any type. When these organizational policies can be made more accommodating or create more employment safety during suffering, they are significant compassion moves.

RITUALS, MEMORIALS, AND MEMENTOS

A final set of compassion moves focuses on improvised compassionate actions that generate resources that are highly customized to the needs and preferences of those who are suffering. We will focus much more on the collective processes that generate significant resources to alleviate suffering in the next section of the book, where we look at organizational competence. Here, we simply want to note that these improvised moves to generate resources are a significant form of compassion at work. Sometimes compassion moves can involve raising money or collecting donations on behalf of someone who is suffering, when those resources will truly help. At other times, compassion moves can involve bringing people together in memorial services, moments of silence, or other rituals that acknowledge suffering. In Nazima's case, she spoke with Ed about wanting something unique to offer as part of Faith's memorial service, but she was not expecting her colleagues to participate.

Ed decided to engage others at work in creating a surprise offering of compassion for Nazima and her family. Together with others at work, Ed designed a ritual that would generate a meaningful memento to share with Nazima that could be incorporated into Faith's memorial service.

Ed and others talked to the organization's leader, who lived in Hawaii and had a profound respect for Hawaiian culture and rituals. The leader helped organize a remembrance ritual for Faith. To perform the ritual, a group of Nazima's colleagues in Hawaii paddled into a calm bay where a Hawaiian elder performed a ceremony for Faith. Recalling their wishes for Nazima and her family, each colleague was asked to gently lift the ring of flowers he or she was wearing and place it on the water. As the flowers floated gently on the surface, a professional underwater photographer captured the ritual and the offering of flowers. After the ritual, the organization sent the beautiful photographs to Nazima and her family to use in the memorial service. This highly improvisational, creative, customized move generated an expression of compassion that remained deeply meaningful to Nazima, years later.

While it can seem as if there is nothing we can do in the face of huge losses such as the death of a child, Ed's consistent compassion moves indicate otherwise. He offered Nazima immediate flexible time to cope with suffering. He created flexibility in Nazima's tasks and became a buffer by engaging others to work through him. He extended generous interpretations of Nazima's absences and reassured her of her job safety during her need to be absent from work. He checked in regularly, expressed concern, and listened with empathy. In the end, Ed was able to expand his personal compassion moves to involve others in a ritual that allowed many colleagues to express their compassion as well.

KEY POINTS: A RANGE OF COMPASSION MOVES AT WORK

∞ Compassionate action is improvisational in that it entails action created on the spot and directed by what is most useful for people who are suffering.

∞ Skillful compassion *moves* are a form of practical knowing-in-action that address suffering and also keep work going.

∞ A range of compassion moves are common at work, including flexible time to cope with suffering, buffering someone from task overload, monitoring and checking in, generating resources that will alleviate suffering, and designing rituals that convey support.

DILEMMAS OF COMPASSIONATE ACTION

For Sethi, who'd been through organizational downturns in the past, the signs were everywhere that life at work was not going to be the same. Top leadership had been saying for months that new technologies were going to change the shape of the business. Sethi, a plant manager at a photographic supply manufacturer, was pretty sure that this was management code for "Watch out, layoffs ahead."

As he had feared, two weeks later Sethi was asked to meet with the regional manager, who told him to eliminate 20 percent of his hourly workforce over the next three months. Sales were down, technology had been purchased that could replace the labor of many of the workers Sethi supervised, and the downsizing would allow the organization to remain profitable in the face of reduced demand. Sethi had no choice about whether or not to comply; the requirements were clear and the mandate given. He felt that he had a dilemma, however, because while he felt he had no choice about the layoff, he also cared about people's well-being. Many managers like Sethi have minimal control over the way in which layoffs are executed. After submitting his list of employees ranked according to their most recent performance review, Sethi watched as a number of human resources employees pulled the plant staff into two separate meetings. In one meeting, those whose jobs had been spared were informed of the downsizing and asked to report back to work. In the other meeting, those whose jobs had been eliminated were informed of their fate and escorted out of the building. The organization's lack of consideration of compassion in the way the downsizing was conducted limited Sethi's options and made it difficult for him to show his concern.

COMPASSION MOVES DURING DOWNSIZING OR JOB LOSS

Downsizing and layoffs of any kind create pain for those whose jobs are eliminated and for those who survive. Research documents responses that range from anxiety, depression, and anger to distraction and health risks.[2] In cases like Sethi's, suffering begets more suffering. For those who are let go, the loss and isolation feeds into destructive health behaviors such as increased smoking and drinking, while new forms of stress arise from financial insecurity, guilt, and shame.[3] Those who remain aren't immune from destructive feelings such as remorse and regret, as well as increased stress at work as they struggle to make sense of what has happened and handle the increased work demands.

Because we have emphasized examples that show skilled moves that build on people's intuitive capacity for compassion, we run the risk of creating an impression that compassion at work is always present or easy. In fact, compassion moves are rarely obvious or easy. As in Sethi's case, significant organizational constraints sometimes prevent managers or coworkers from being able to engage in some types of compassionate action. Researchers investigate methods by which managers can perform what they call "necessary evils" with greater compassion, showing that greater care in the process makes a significant difference.[4] While organizations often choose to perform layoffs in a perfunctory way because of legal concerns, compassion in the process can make a significant difference in people's mental and emotional outcomes. Managers who meet personally with those who are leaving and who express compassion for their circumstances reduce the suffering. Likewise, managers who address the loss and suffering with those who remain, and who make space for discussion of what has happened, encourage compassion that alleviates some of the feelings of being isolated, alone, and bereft. One employee in our research who was let go from a position with compassion during a downsizing process commented, "I am interested in how an organization accomplished a layoff in a thoughtful and respectful way and established some degree of security despite the changes. I wish more organizations handled layoffs like this."

The lack of compassion in most downsizing practices exacerbates the financial suffering by adding emotional costs. It doesn't have to be this way. Legalistic approaches to human suffering create compassion dilemmas that are costly. For instance, physicians used to be coached not to apologize for things that went wrong in a medical procedure because of the fear of lawsuits, creating compassion dilemmas for doctors who wanted to connect with patients in the face of suffering. Researchers who examine malpractice lawsuits have found that this legalistic approach exacerbates rather than solves the problem. When physicians or administrators address suffering and apologize for errors, the number of lawsuits decreases.[5] Likewise with layoffs. While managers are routinely coached not to apologize or address suffering, research on downsizing shows us that when this process is done with compassion, it increases the organization's profitability along with well-being and resilience for both those who are leaving and those left behind.

COMPASSION MOVES TO ADDRESS TOXICITY
AND DESTIGMATIZE SUFFERING

As we saw when we discussed the costs of empathy in chapter 5, managers or others may feel there is a dilemma in acting with compassion because the job of alleviating suffering seems too big, too uncertain, or too demanding. Research validates the idea that when managers and colleagues do open up space for compassionate conversation, even in the face of toxic politics, poor performance, or other difficult-to-address forms of workplace suffering, others respond. These compassion moves are what our CompassionLab cofounder, Peter Frost, referred to as "toxin handling."[6] When work is creating suffering, these people voluntarily serve as peacemakers, listeners, and healers in relation to work conflicts, as Veronica did with Rosita and Juana. They overcome the dilemma by intervening to alleviate suffering associated with work tasks and work relationships. Toxin handling is often invisible in the wider view of the organization, but it is potent in awakening compassion in our work lives. Peter found these compassion moves so powerful that he called for toxin handling to be recognized as a formal role in organizations and to be rewarded for the difficult work it entails. The compassion moves that address toxicity at work—challenging and often thankless—keep the human community on the mend.

Workplace suffering sometimes comes from being ignored or overlooked as much as from being treated with disrespect. Many organizations create compassion dilemmas because they have a way of treating low-status people as invisible. In the face of this fact, powerful compassion moves often involve extending compassion not just to high-status employees but also to those who make the copies or sweep the floors. Compassion moves that extend recognition and benefits to low-status employees are important in alleviating suffering that is widespread and helping resolve this compassion dilemma. Work that is stigmatized or somehow perceived to be "dirty work" in an organization can block compassion as well. As described by Jeff, a member of the janitorial and maintenance staff in an organization we studied, there were many ways that compassionate actions fell short simply because of his role: "After working in maintenance for over five years, I have not seen *any* sign of compassion in this workplace. Even when both of my in-laws passed away, flowers, cards, even a word of sympathy was never received. When my child was born, no sign of any type was seen, flowers, card, congrats—nothing." When colleagues and managers limit compassion moves toward those in stigmatized or low-status occupations, suffering escalates. It is not always easy to ensure that compassionate action reaches every corner of an organization, but resolving these dilemmas in favor of greater dignity and inclusion is an indicator of greater compassion competence in the whole organization.

COMPASSION MOVES TO PROTECT PRIVACY

A different type of compassion dilemma arises when organizations, managers, or coworkers need to protect the privacy of those who are suffering even as they figure out how to take compassionate action. Some instances that call for compassionate action at work are murky and difficult, and not everyone will want his or her suffering acknowledged in public. Research now validates the fact that receiving compassion is often accompanied by a variety of fears, exacerbating these dilemmas and making compassion moves even more difficult.[7] Suffering entails vulnerability, and people may not want to risk being seen as weak.[8] Some people conflate compassion with pity and reject it because they feel shame. These compassion dilemmas arose for Krista and Liam, whom we met in our research. Krista used improvisational moves to focus on compassion at work even while protecting Liam's privacy.

Liam had already given two weeks' notice and resigned from the manufacturing plant where he had worked for a few years as a line leader when his partner, Nathan, started to complain that he was too tired to go to work. While Nathan was ill, Liam made soup and drove their kids to school and coached soccer, keeping their lives normal. After a week of Nathan being unable to rise to the demands of their busy life with three young boys, Liam persuaded Nathan to see a doctor. Nathan did not recover. Inconclusive tests piled up, as did medical bills that began to worry Liam. How would he be able to take on a new job with this strain from Nathan's illness?

When Liam and the shift foreman asked Krista, the human resources leader, to join their meeting one morning just before Liam's departure, she was surprised. Liam's work transition plan was in order, and she couldn't imagine what else was needed. The shift foreman shocked Krista by asking her to rescind Liam's letter of resignation. Without going into detail, he explained that Liam's partner was suffering from a protracted undiagnosed illness and Liam needed continuous insurance coverage. Krista recalled the careful attention that the shift foreman gave to talking with her while protecting Liam and Nathan's privacy, not putting Liam on the spot or revealing too many details.

The ambiguous nature of Nathan's illness, coupled with Liam's desire to keep his situation private, made it difficult to interpret Liam's needs. No one wanted to ask too many questions, but Krista and the other leaders recognized that one thing they could do was to interpret this suffering in a generous way and extend Liam's employment status. They rescinded his resignation. That decision provided stable employment and health insurance to the family, an expression of the organization's compassion. Krista conveyed how she put herself in Liam's shoes during this time as a way to tap into her feelings of concern: "If you can imagine trying to change benefit providers in the middle of something like that, well, it's just really stressful."

Liam feared that his coworkers' judgment about his life outside of work could create discord, so he kept his life with Nathan and their kids very private. After a few weeks, Nathan was diagnosed with a very rare form of terminal cancer that was untreatable. Krista recalled the dilemma she felt: "I wanted to do something. I never had a close relationship with Liam, but I wanted to do something. But I also knew that he didn't want to be involved." When word circled the work community that Nathan would soon die, Krista knew that others would share her desire to respond. She described her thought process at the time: "I felt sure that there would be a variety of emotions among our staff. Something like this is scary and sad. So I considered what we could do to create space for people to have whatever emotions they had. I wanted to honor Liam and Nathan, but also to create a community together for everyone else at work."

Krista had attended a Quaker college, and the rituals from that institution inspired her as she wrestled with the dilemma of how to respond to Nathan's terminal illness. She recalled, "In college, whenever we had a crisis or there was a difficult situation in the world, we would gather in the heart of the campus—metaphorically and literally gather around the heart—and form a massive circle for a moment of silence. It occurred to me that this could be a beautiful way to come together, acknowledge Liam and Nathan, and reinforce our community. So I checked with the plant manager. He thought it was a good idea, and then I sent a message inviting the entire shift to attend during lunch break."

Rituals like this one are often helpful in times when people need to find their way into shared humanity that fuels more generous interpretations in the face of suffering. While work can become a world of rational action, moments of grief, loss, and shock often call for rituals that bring us back to our common roots. On a day when Liam was not present, Krista and her organization gathered in an empty space on the factory floor at the lunch break. Krista said a few words of introduction to the circle and invited people to be silent together and to call to mind Liam and Nathan if they wished. The Quaker tradition offers that people only need to speak if they feel that they can improve upon the silence. Krista and her plant manager held the circle until the plant manager closed with an invitation to remain for lunch together. "There were a lot of tears and hugs and connections," Krista remembered. "It just allowed people to be together to feel whatever they felt. I was surprised when I walked in to see a lot of people from the night shift there, too," she said. "Apparently, staff had shared the invitation. Afterward, many of them thanked me for the opportunity to be present, remarking on how important it was for them to feel that we were coming together as a community."

Krista's invitation to her workplace to come together in a deliberate moment of silence fostered feelings of gratitude from many members of the organization, who didn't know exactly what else to do for Liam and Nathan. The dilemma of acknowledging suffering while preserving privacy was resolved by the ritual that Krista facilitated. She and others wrote an account of their feelings as they stood in the circle and later shared it with Liam as a token of their sympathy. When leaders like Krista find ways to improvise compassion moves that bring people together without sacrificing someone's wishes to be alone, these moves help workplace communities engage in alleviating suffering with integrity and dignity.

KEY POINTS: DILEMMAS OF COMPASSIONATE ACTION

∞ Dilemmas arise when compassion is hindered by legalistic approaches that deny human connection. Compassion moves restore warmth.

∞ Corrosive politics, toxic interactions, consistent underperformance, and other forms of conflict at work are significant sources of suffering that cannot be left unaddressed. They require fierce compassion.

∞ Dilemmas arise when people fear giving or receiving compassion at work because of being viewed as weak or vulnerable. Compassion moves remain sensitive to these fears and preserve integrity and privacy.

AN INVITATION TO REFLECT ON COMPASSION MOVES

Suffering ripples across an organization in ways that aren't predictable. Improvised compassionate action meets it, calling people into a flow that evolves as needs become clear. When actions to alleviate suffering are improvisational, wise, and creative, they become compassion moves that represent practical knowing-in-action. Compassion moves take into account the hierarchies and power structures that otherwise hinder our capacity to see one another, creating flexibility and time to heal even as work moves ahead. Compassion moves draw us together, renewing human connection in rituals that offer solace. While in the grind of time, organizations grip us with task demands, deadlines, and performance pressures, compassion moves buffer us and create spaciousness to awaken our capacity for compassion even as we keep work going.

When have you improvised in the face of suffering or faced down a dilemma of compassionate action at work? Use the tool in Part Four: Blueprints for Awakening Compassion at Work to discover your strengths and weaknesses and to build your capacity for compassion at work.

PART THREE

AWAKENING COMPASSION
COMPETENCE IN
ORGANIZATIONS

In this section, we move beyond individual responses to suffering and take a system-level perspective, looking at elements of organizations and how workplaces can be designed with compassion in mind.

This section opens a window into how leaders, managers, employees, and change agents—the compassion architects of an organization—can awaken compassion competence across entire systems. Rather than focusing on how individuals respond to suffering, we focus on how whole organizations respond. We will show you what compassion competence looks like in different kinds of organizations and reveal a framework for understanding generally what contributes to compassion competence in a system. We refer to this framework as the *social architecture* of an organization, defined as a unique amalgam of the social network structures that link people together, the culture of a workplace, the ways that work roles are defined, the ways that leaders' actions and stories model and give meaning to compassion, and the ways that routine work is accomplished.

We will explain the social architecture framework in detail in chapter 8 and show how it informs a set of design principles for creating compassion in organizations in chapter 9. Our research demonstrates that all these elements of a system make a difference in our capacity to awaken compassion in organizations. Let's see how, by starting with one elaborate case study that brings to life the idea of compassion competence in organizations.

7

ENVISIONING
COMPASSION
COMPETENCE

GIVEN THAT COMPASSION IS an interpersonal process, how does an entire organization awaken compassion? Let's take a look at the interpersonal model we introduced in the first section of the book and build on it. In our research, we have shown that the compassion competence of a system depends *on an emergent pattern of collective noticing, interpreting, feeling, and acting in an effective and customized fashion in order to alleviate suffering.* Two points warrant further exploration to help us envision compassion competence. First, this definition hinges on collective and coordinated *emergent patterns*, meaning that the process takes shape across many people and actions and is not determined in advance. A new pattern emerges when suffering surfaces in an organization. Some are simple, others are intricate—competence in the system shapes the pattern in relation to the unique needs of people who are suffering.

Second, this is a definition of compassion *competence*—it includes the assumption that compassion must be shaped in relation to suffering in a customized way in order to be effective. Patterns that fail to meet the needs of those who are suffering don't rise to the level of compassion competence. Patterns that fail to generate resources to alleviate suffering likewise fail to rise to the level of competence. We will describe four important dimensions of compassion competence derived from our research and show you how leaders, managers, employees, and change agents at all levels can use these measures to awaken greater compassion competence in their organizations.[1]

COMPASSION COMPETENCE AT TECHCO

Zeke was enjoying an unusual moment of solitude as he biked through the park on a bright autumn day. He didn't have many opportunities to take his mountain bike out now, since he traveled almost every week for his job as a sales representative at TechCo. Zeke had joined the regional office of this large multinational technology organization in Haifa, Israel, just over a year ago. Getting used to his travel schedule combined with adjusting to life with a new baby kept him fully occupied. But today his wife, Geet, had encouraged him to take his bike and get outside. Zeke's father, Ezra, and brother, Eli, were visiting, and the new grandfather and uncle were keen for time with the baby. Their apartment overlooked a park where Zeke could ride easily without being gone too long. Ezra urged Zeke out the door. "Geet can get some rest," he said, "and you go enjoy the day."

Rounding a bend and riding downhill toward home, Zeke felt a strange stiffening in his leg. He didn't know what was happening to him. He lost the ability to control his legs as the bike was gathering speed quickly down the hill. The stiffening of his legs and his sudden inability to move did not allow him to manipulate the pedals. He grasped at the brake, but he couldn't control the bike. It careened downhill, tumbling over and over. The bright autumn day melted around Zeke as his consciousness seeped away.

Geet happened to be looking out the window at that moment, watching for Zeke to come home. She saw the bike flip and tumble. She called out, and Ezra and Eli raced from the apartment toward the park. When they got to Zeke, he was not breathing. Ezra and Eli wiped away blood and sand to make room to open Zeke's airway. They performed CPR until the ambulance arrived. The emergency responders lifted Zeke onto a backboard and moved him quickly.

Little did Zeke know that this terrible accident would launch him, his family, and his workplace into an extraordinary story of organizational compassion competence. We have changed names and a few identifying details of this case, but like the other examples in this book, Zeke's story isn't invented. Zeke and other members of his organization recounted this case to us when we were investigating what organizational scholars refer to as *positive deviant* cases of compassion competence across an entire system.[2] If *positive deviance* sounds like a contradiction in terms, it isn't. It simply means that organizations or systems can deviate from the norm or from what might be expected compared with the tendencies of many organizations in ways that are dramatically excellent (positive deviance) or dramatically dysfunctional (negative deviance). In relation to safety, for instance, some organizations are negatively deviant, meaning that they have far more accidents and safety violations than most organizations. Others are positively deviant, meaning that they have very few accidents or safety violations. Research on compassion in organizations shows that some organizations perpetuate suffering to a great degree (negative deviance), some do relatively little to alleviate suffering, and some have designed systems that enable them to do many things to foster healing (positive deviance).[3] We study positively deviant organizations like TechCo to understand how they accomplish this high level of compassion competence.

SPEED AND TIME CONTRIBUTE TO COMPASSION COMPETENCE

Zeke's work community shared strong bonds. They responded almost immediately when they found out about his accident. Ezra phoned Avi, Zeke's manager, who let the rest of his team know that Zeke had been taken to the emergency room. Although it was a weekend, members of Zeke's work team arrived at the hospital right away, filling the waiting room even before Zeke regained consciousness. Looking through the lens of an organization's social architecture, we can see that Zeke's colleagues in the Haifa office were highly interconnected by high-quality social ties in their work network. TechCo culture features explicit values of respecting and caring for each other that were put into action by Zeke's work team.

In relation to compassion competence, *speed* is defined as the timing and rhythm of actions that address suffering. Greater speed is an indicator of compassion competence, and speed can be measured in two ways. First, *immediacy* means that organizations can spring into action quickly and respond effectively to the shock of suffering caused by an unexpected trauma or loss. Second, speed also refers to adjustments over time. *Competence* means that organizations can speedily shift what they are doing and quickly make adjustments as what is necessary comes into view.

THE VALUE OF IMMEDIACY

TechCo mobilized many resources quickly to address the suffering of Zeke and his family, not least of which was the comfort of Zeke's colleagues' immediate presence. Beyond that, one of Zeke's team members brought an extra prepaid cell phone and gave it to Geet for the family's use. Zeke's coworkers brought food for those in the waiting room. As they waited to understand Zeke's condition, Geet and Ezra received a call from Raoul, the vice president of TechCo's European and Middle Eastern operations, the division governing the Israel sales office. After the call from Ezra, Zeke's manager, Avi, had issued an immediate alert to executives across TechCo, which was standard practice after a major injury or illness of an employee. This alert got Raoul's attention and allowed him to quickly tap into resources across a broader network of people within the organization. Looking again through the lens of TechCo's social architecture, we see that activating the regional and division networks that tied people together across the organization greatly enhanced TechCo's speedy response. The standardization of alerts about significant sources of suffering such as injury and illness contributed to the speed of this call from Raoul. The call also included reassurances to the family that Zeke's job was secure and that TechCo would support them.

ADJUSTING OVER TIME

In gauging compassion competence, immediacy isn't the only temporal marker that counts. A competent response can also require sustained adjustments over time, which demands ongoing attention to suffering, interpretations of changing conditions, extended feelings of concern, and ongoing coordinated actions. Many criticisms of compassion in the wake of natural disasters, for instance, focus on the lack of sustained responsiveness as needs shift from the immediate crisis to the challenges of longer-term rebuilding and recovery. In the face of large-scale suffering, competence can falter when systems fail to sustain the capability to quickly adjust their responses over time.[4]

At TechCo, we will see that compassion competence involved sustained attention for Zeke and his family, ongoing interpretations of their condition, elaborated empathy and concern, and the rapid coordination of many compassionate actions over a long time period. Zeke's hospitalization was extensive. His coworkers coordinated a schedule for visiting that spanned months. This pattern meant that there was almost always someone on hand who could run an errand, hold the baby, listen, or sit and talk. Avi and Zeke's other work colleagues remained attuned to Geet, Ezra, and Zeke's needs, just as they had in the beginning of Zeke's hospitalization, and used their inquiry work as well as their presence and empathic concern to pick up clues about what might be most helpful as Zeke's condition changed.

KEY POINTS: SPEED AND COMPASSION COMPETENCE

∞ Speed, defined as the timing and rhythm of actions that address suffering, is one measure of the compassion competence of an organization.

∞ One dimension of speed involves immediacy: how quickly a compassionate response begins to unfold following an episode of suffering.

∞ Another dimension of speed involves sustaining compassionate actions over time and continuing to quickly adjust as conditions change.

SCOPE OF RESOURCES CONTRIBUTES TO COMPASSION COMPETENCE

The breadth of resources called upon to alleviate suffering forms a second measure of compassion competence. In Zeke's case, the extensive surgery that had been performed immediately after his accident was not successful. His surgeon told Ezra and Geet that Zeke might not walk again. When Raoul called to check in with them and learned of Zeke's condition, he told Geet, "I just want you to know that we've given instructions to your local office to do whatever they can to support you. And I am going to call each day to check on Zeke's progress. If you need anything, please call me. Here's my direct number." A little while later, Geet received a call from Barbara, the vice president of human resources at TechCo headquarters in the United States. She repeated what Raoul had offered and said that she could be reached at any time. Looking through the lens of TechCo's social architecture, which helps us see with more technical precision what is making a difference in organizations, we can see that these executives deployed communication routines that were designed to enhance compassion competence in the system by facilitating the flow of information. In addition, we can see how these leaders' actions made the organizational values of respect and care come alive at all organizational levels, contributing to compassion competence in the system overall.

SCOPE IS MEASURED BY BREADTH OF RESOURCES

When we take a system view of compassion, we see that alleviating suffering requires the generation of resources. When we say resources, however, we don't just mean material goods or money, we mean *anything that can be put to use to alleviate suffering.*[5] We measure compassion competence in part by the breadth or scope of resources an organization devotes to alleviating suffering.

This way of thinking about resources shifts from a focus on inherent value (such as dollars) toward a focus on how a wide variety of actions and things take on value as they are put to use to alleviate suffering.[6] In Zeke's case, we can see a wide breadth of resources, including the physical and psychological presence of coworkers, the attention of managers and other leaders, acts of empathic listening, words that conveyed emotional concern, supportive reassurance, flexible time for Zeke's recovery, meals, a cell phone, help running errands, child care—and the list goes on.

Looking again through the lens of TechCo's social architecture, we see that the attention of the regional and global executives was not just nice to have; it was a resource that fueled compassion competence. While Barbara and Raoul reassured Geet and Ezra, they also used their attention to unlock other kinds of resources within TechCo, such as added insurance coverage. And they helped unlock significant financial aid, as we will see later, in conjunction with employees in TechCo worldwide. Leaders are important in the social architecture of compassion because they are models for behavior and can use positions of power to mobilize many other kinds of resources that can alleviate suffering. The breadth of resources that marked TechCo's high level of competence was enhanced not just by the improvised actions of local employees but also by networks of leaders and others who participated in spreading the pattern all around the world.

SCOPE REQUIRES CALIBRATION

To create positively deviant compassion competence is no simple task. And organizations must generate a wide breadth of resources and calibrate the variety to the unique needs of those who are suffering. Too many resources that aren't useful can undermine competence instead of enhance it. For instance, in Zeke's case, the donation of material goods was not useful because Zeke had to transfer to different hospitals for more experimental clinical treatments, and it was difficult for his family to manage too many material things in the moves. TechCo calibrated the breadth of resources that it offered with what remained useful to Zeke and his family as conditions changed. Employees continued to visit, to run errands and provide help with child care, and to offer consistent expressions of empathic concern and words of comfort. But they also added to this breadth by providing coordination help to move Zeke into different care facilities, making arrangements for new forms of insurance coverage, and investigating new treatments. The sustained attention and generous interpretations of Zeke's condition as it changed helped TechCo to calibrate the breadth of resources to Zeke's needs. Zeke and his family told us that the scope of resources offered to them and how the pattern was calibrated with what was useful to them made them feel as though they were being swept up in a tidal wave of affection that helped them heal.

KEY POINTS: SCOPE OF RESOURCES AND COMPASSION COMPETENCE

- ∞ The scope of resources is defined by breadth. A broad array of resources that can be mobilized to alleviate suffering provides a measure of compassion competence.

- ∞ Resources as they relate to compassion competence are defined as anything that can be put to use to alleviate suffering.

- ∞ Common resources mobilized by organizations include presence, empathic listening, running errands, providing child care, words of comfort, tangible goods such as meals or clothing or household items, flexible time arrangements, and money.

- ∞ Scope must be calibrated to what is useful as needs change over time.

MAGNITUDE OF RESOURCES CONTRIBUTES TO COMPASSION COMPETENCE

In his conversations with Ezra, Avi picked up on small clues that Ezra was feeling anxious about having enough money to cover the costs of a set of expensive experimental clinical trials. These experimental treatments offered a small but significant chance for Zeke to regain use of his legs. Wondering about this one morning, Avi asked Ezra to sit with him in a quiet corner of the waiting room. "I am thinking about Zeke's expenses," he confided, "and I cannot imagine that the insurance will pay for all that Zeke needs with these new treatments." Ezra felt his shoulders rise with tension. Avi continued, "I do not want to insult Geet or Zeke. But do you think that they would be willing to accept a donation, if we find a way to raise money?"

Avi engaged in skilled inquiry work in this conversation, using his questions about a potential need to explore what would be useful in a respectful manner. Avi's inquiry work allowed Ezra to keep his financial situation private and to decline the offer of a donation if it was not welcome. Avi's example shows the ongoing need for generous interpretations of new forms of suffering that arise as conditions change. Ezra's worried manner was a clue that Avi picked up on, and his willingness to inquire and to offer a generous interpretation of Ezra's suffering opened the door to a new wave of coordinated compassionate actions at TechCo.

INCREASING THE AMOUNT OF RESOURCES TO ALLEVIATE SUFFERING

One aspect of magnitude simply refers to the amount of resources generated by a system to direct toward alleviating suffering. At TechCo, Avi began choreographing another pattern in the elaborate dance by alerting the human resources leader in his local office to his desire to begin accumulating funds for Zeke. In response, TechCo suggested activating its vacation-time-donation policy, which enabled people to donate the value of their unused vacation time to Zeke. This policy applied to all TechCo divisions around the world. Zeke's coworkers began spreading the call for help to anyone they knew in TechCo who might be willing to donate. They wrote a story about Zeke for the TechCo employee spotlight newsletter, asking for donations. Money poured in from TechCo employees worldwide, providing Zeke and Geet with a significant amount of financial aid right away.

Avi also reached out again to Raoul, asking that the European and Middle East division of TechCo provide matching funds for all the money donated by TechCo employees in Israel. Avi knew, based on past experience with Raoul, that the trust and respect that existed between units would make this achievement seem important and urgent. Raoul approved Avi's request right away. TechCo's Europe and Middle East division matched the funds raised by Zeke's coworkers in Israel. This matching fund greatly increased the amount of money available for Zeke's ongoing treatment. Raoul in turn reached out to Barbara to convey the size of Zeke's expenses. Barbara approached the CEO of TechCo to approve a matching grant from the US headquarters for a portion of the money that had been donated by employees across TechCo. TechCo's CEO personally reviewed the case and approved the additional matching grant.

Looking through the lens of TechCo's social architecture, we can see that the magnitude of financial resources TechCo mobilized was enhanced by organizational routines for donating unused vacation time and converting it to cash. This organizational routine is now widespread, and many organizations allow employees to use this sort of policy to alleviate suffering. At TechCo, additional routines for using pools of money from the organization's human resources budgets to match employee donations further enlarged the pool of resources. The trust that existed in the network ties between managers and executives at various levels all across TechCo further enhanced the magnitude of resources, because generosity was met with generosity rather than with mistrust. Altogether this created a pattern in which employees at all levels of TechCo, spanning all the way from the CEO to engineers in India to the receptionist in the Israel office, participated in alleviating the suffering of financial strain for Zeke's family and enabling Zeke to continue to seek the best treatments available.

MATCHING MAGNITUDE TO NEED

It would be a mistake to say that greater magnitude *by itself* is always a marker of compassion competence. When the magnitude of resources overwhelms the capability of people to use them, more resources actually can be a hindrance to compassion competence. Compassion scholars Dean Williams and Trent Shepherd have studied how local ventures spring up in the wake of large disasters in order to add to the competence of local systems. These new ventures often try to match the large magnitude of resources that are donated immediately after a disaster with people who can use them. Without this matching, resources simply go unused, increasing waste and lowering the competence of the overall system. So in relation to compassion competence, another aspect of magnitude involves how well matched the amount of resources is to the needs of those who are suffering.

At TechCo, the magnitude of financial resources wasn't wasteful or extravagant. It was matched to the extraordinary level of expense involved in Zeke's treatment and recovery. Ezra, Geet, and Zeke were stunned by TechCo's generosity. It helped them to see the values of the organization in action. As Zeke described, "I think that the company instills a sense of responsibility for healing or compassion to employees through the personal examples of the management. I have seen that from the day I joined the company."

KEY POINTS: MAGNITUDE OF RESOURCES AND COMPASSION COMPETENCE

- ∞ The magnitude of resources that are generated by an organization in order to alleviate suffering is one measure of compassion competence.

- ∞ Magnitude involves not only the amount of resources but also how well those resources are matched to the changing needs of those who are suffering.

- ∞ While the existence of too few resources is a marker of incompetence, having too many resources that are not matched with people's needs can exacerbate suffering rather than alleviate it.

CUSTOMIZATION CONTRIBUTES TO COMPASSION COMPETENCE

Many organizations have a relatively simple and standard repertoire of responses to difficult or painful life events—perhaps sending flowers when someone is ill or feeling blue, sending flowers when a pet dies, and sending flowers when there is a death in the family. While a symbolic expression of concern is welcome and meaningful, the fact that the same repertoire is deployed in response to quite different episodes of suffering can be a marker of low competence. To achieve high levels of compassion competence, organizations must enable complex and novel repertoires. When they do, a system is capable of generating idiosyncratic and highly individualized resources to alleviate suffering, which is what we mean when we refer to customization of resources as the fourth measure of compassion competence.

TechCo offers an example of the opposite of simple and standard response repertoires. Rather than one kind of action or resource, TechCo employees engaged in an elaborately coordinated, complex repertoire of actions that generated highly individualized resources for Zeke. For instance, after one of the experimental surgeries enabled Zeke to regain feeling in his legs, he moved from a hospital to a rehabilitation center where he could engage in physical therapy and strengthening. In the rehab center, TechCo built him a customized workstation and Avi arranged for a modified laptop computer and a secure network connection. All the while, Zeke's coworkers continued their visits and elaborated on their compassionate actions. During one visit to the rehab center, Zeke's colleagues realized that there was not going to be a Hanukkah party. Later that month, they showed up with candles, food, drinks, games, desserts, and decorations and threw a Hanukkah party for all the residents.

The first time Zeke logged in to his email, he discovered a personal message from the CEO of TechCo wishing him well. He found personal messages from the global, regional, and local human resources leaders and many others in the organization. People across TechCo who had heard of Zeke's condition had written words of comfort and good wishes for his recovery. Avi began to prepare for Zeke to return to work full-time. TechCo commissioned new equipment for Zeke's office. The human resources team secured a transfer for Zeke from a role that had required a great deal of travel to a similar role that could be done primarily from his local office. Since he would sometimes need to meet with clients, TechCo secured a company car outfitted with appropriate hand-operated technology so that Zeke could drive.

Seen through the lens of TechCo's social architecture, the generation of highly customized resources relies on an amalgam of many elements of the organization, such as social networks imbued with trust and cultural values that emphasize care put into action by managers like Avi, who envisioned his role as a manager in ways that encompassed compassionate action for Zeke as part of his normal work responsibilities. Long after these events, Zeke told us that the constant presence and care expressed by his coworkers was deeply meaningful. It blended with other resources such as the money and customized return-to-work equipment to inspire him even in the dark times. He said, "I feel that TechCo helped me a lot through this rough time. It was encouraging and inspiring to see my friends from work calling and visiting. I think that the fact that I knew that they would continue to visit, and that I would return to work for TechCo, provided a lot of very much needed peace of mind."

CUSTOMIZED RESOURCES AREN'T ALWAYS EXPENSIVE

Learning about TechCo and its response to Zeke might create the impression that highly customized resources are always as expensive as a specially outfitted car or workstation. But that is not the case. Customized resources come in all shapes and sizes. One organization we studied regularly created unique handmade cards for people in distress. In this pattern, upon learning about a difficulty or a source of suffering in someone's life, one member would begin a folded paper card and pass it around the organization. Others knew the pattern and added materials and words to the card. What started as simple folded paper was passed from person to person, each member adding something witty, supportive, or creative. We saw ingenious use of bandages, pennies, paper clips, dollar bills, pressed flowers, drawings, magazine clippings, and innumerable small items incorporated into the cards. They became treasured expressions of compassion. Because they were created in direct response to a specific episode of suffering using the organization's knowledge of a colleague's likes, dislikes, sense of humor, and so on, these inexpensive customized resources took on great value.

KEY POINTS: CUSTOMIZATION OF RESOURCES AND COMPASSION COMPETENCE

∞ The customization of resources, how individualized they are to unique needs and preferences, is a measure of compassion competence.

∞ Many organizations have simple, rote repertoires for responding to suffering, such as sending flowers. These generate resources but do not do much to customize them.

∞ Customized resources, while individualized, need not be expensive.

AN INVITATION TO REFLECT ON COMPASSION COMPETENCE

Zeke's story and TechCo's response help us to envision compassion competence in an organization. Many of us have not had an experience of a workplace like Zeke's or been swept up in the coordinated effort of an extraordinarily competent compassionate system. We need new ways to imagine what's possible. Examples like TechCo help us to see in a whole new way what we mean by an *emergent pattern of collective noticing, interpreting, feeling, and acting in an effective and customized fashion in order to alleviate suffering.* Far beyond any one person, this pattern involves many people and resources in responding to suffering.

We also need examples like TechCo to illuminate how the structures and processes of an organization contribute to collective patterns of response to suffering. A social architecture like TechCo's takes a spark of concern and breathes it into a fire of compassionate action. That is no accident—it is a competent pattern of compassionate action, deliberately created by many people but not controlled by anyone. This emergent pattern is fragile but meaningful. It helps us to see the immense capacity of organizations to alleviate suffering.

How does a story like the TechCo case spark your imagination about what is possible for compassion competence in your organization?

8

UNDERSTANDING COMPASSION COMPETENCE

ALTHOUGH ZEKE WAS IN A relatively low-level sales position in a far-flung subsidiary office of a multinational corporation, TechCo swung into action immediately upon his hospitalization. Over a period of months and across a span of geography, this organization and its members engaged in an extraordinary pattern of collective noticing, interpreting, feeling, and acting to alleviate Zeke's suffering in whatever ways they could. To some, it may seem unusual that an organization would go to such lengths for one employee. Yet we know from our research that TechCo engaged in patterns of compassion competence regularly and consistently. Employees suffering from different kinds of losses and setbacks, working in all kinds of positions, and located all around the world experienced the power of compassion at TechCo. While each pattern encompasses different details, what they have in common is the competence enabled by TechCo's social architecture that allowed for a high degree of calibration of resources with needs, matching the breadth to what was most useful, and customizing them to the individuality of people who were suffering.

TechCo's capacity to respond to the suffering of not just Zeke but also thousands of other employees in a unique, individualized, competent manner animates our ability to imagine how we might design organizations that excel at compassion competence. Of course, TechCo was not perfect. Some employees experienced compassion lacking even in this highly competent organization. But if you think Zeke's story is too good to be true, we encourage you to realize that there are many others like it. In this chapter, we want to revisit some elements of the TechCo case to reveal more about what enabled the organization to create reliable and repeated patterns of compassion in response to multiple episodes of suffering. Let's explore a framework that helps us to more deeply understand what enables compassion competence in organizations.

A SOCIAL ARCHITECTURE FRAMEWORK

Awakening compassion competence in organizations goes beyond individual hearts and minds—it requires the fundamental building blocks of organizational life. In our research, we have identified elements of organizations that make the biggest difference in a system's ability to achieve highly competent patterns of collective noticing, interpreting, feeling, and responding. We refer to these elements all together as an organization's *social architecture*.[1] The social architecture of an organization is composed of its social network structures and the ways that people are tied together in the system, the culture of the workplace, the ways that work roles are defined, the ways that routine work is accomplished, and the meaning and modeling that leaders provide. Looking at how the social architecture of an organization enables compassion competence helps us to see how structures and processes in work organizations contribute to people's ability to pick up on suffering and create patterns to alleviate it.

One of our goals in illuminating the framework of a social architecture is to help leaders, managers, employees, and change agents to understand what enables organizational compassion competence. These are the system's compassion architects. They design and build the elements that make up the social architecture, and as they do, they exert enormous influence over our expectations of what is appropriate and possible when suffering surfaces at work.

NETWORKS AWAKEN COMPASSION COMPETENCE

Organizations are composed of what sociologist Georg Simmel called *webs of affiliations*, or what are today commonly referred to as *social networks*.[2] When researchers study organizational networks, they point to how repeated social interactions between people form a social structure that governs flows of information and helps determine people's power and influence based on whom they know and interact with on a regular basis.[3] You might have heard of network research in terms of "six degrees of separation," which is a popular way of understanding how many network ties link us with other people and allow us to reach them even if we don't know them well. This is the first aspect of networks that we focus on in relation to compassion competence. Since social networks provide a structure that captures patterns of interactions between people, these networks can be activated in the wake of suffering. Network structures are often depicted in maps that show how regularly people talk or share information or advice with each other, and research also shows how energy and emotion flow through these structures.[4] As in a highway system, feelings, interpretations, and calls for action travel fast on the most established and biggest paths. This is why networks matter so much for how quickly information about suffering is shared and how easy it is to calibrate and coordinate patterns of compassion competence in a system.

Social networks in organizations matter for compassion competence in a second way too. In addition to the structure of the networks, we can look at the *quality* of the interpersonal ties between people. High-quality connections are defined by feelings of mutuality, vitality, and positive regard that flow between people, even in momentary interactions. These connections have strong effects. For instance, when ties are higher in quality, they are more tensile, helping us to be more flexible in responding to one another. High-quality connections also have the capacity to carry more positive and negative emotion with less strain.[5] For example, if someone who is suffering missed a deadline, high-quality connections enable coworkers to express both the negative emotions of displeasure with the missed deadline and positive concern or care without sacrificing the relationship. Jane and her colleagues have researched the energizing effects of high-quality connections at work.[6] Connections like these speed up the flow of information and resources when suffering surfaces because people can rely on the respect and trust they've built in their connections to find ways to improvise together.

In the case of TechCo's social networks, we see structural network effects on competence in the rapid sharing of information and resources between the Haifa office and Europe and Middle East division office. Similar structural effects between Raoul's division and Barbara's division at headquarters kept information and resources flowing. Similarly, when Zeke's coworkers sent out calls for other TechCo employees to participate in the vacation donation program, they tapped into their own social networks to draw even more people into the pattern. We also see that TechCo's network ties are generally infused with a high degree of trust and respect. For instance, the high-quality bonds between Zeke and his teammates amplified the pattern. So did the high-quality connection between Avi and Raoul. Zeke reflected to us that this seemed to characterize many relationships within TechCo: "Although TechCo is a huge, multibillion-dollar company with branches all over the world, I felt that the people I work with really cared about their peers and started to organize on my behalf when I was in the accident. I believe that the close relationships I had with many of the people here is why they reacted this way."

In some organizations, the fact that someone suffered a sudden illness that contributed to a debilitating bicycle accident outside of work on a weekend would not be an organizational event at all—no one would notice or respond. Perhaps the employee would take a leave of absence or maybe just disappear. So why in Zeke's case did his accident become a rallying cry for months of compassionate responses? Network structures in the organization carried information about Zeke's accident and calls for help throughout the organization quickly. Connections characterized by trust helped people to regard the news as credible, amplifying people's attention and responsiveness. In this way, networks and the quality of connections between people provide a central leverage point for designing compassion competence.

KEY POINTS: HOW NETWORKS AWAKEN
COMPASSION COMPETENCE

∞ Organizational social networks create a social structure that ties people together in particular ways.

∞ Network ties provide highways for the flow of information, advice, feelings, and energy. Activating these highways upon learning of suffering is a powerful way to evoke patterns of compassionate action.

∞ The quality of the ties in the networks matters. High-quality connections are more flexible, lending to the capacity to improvise together. They carry more emotion without strain, amplifying feelings of empathy.

∞ Networks contribute to compassion competence by making it faster and easier to communicate and coordinate as well as more likely that people will pay attention and regard notifications about suffering as credible.

ORGANIZATIONAL CULTURE AWAKENS COMPASSION COMPETENCE

Emphasis on the importance of organizational culture has grown, so it is fairly common today to talk about the role of organizational culture in making great places to work. Organizational culture is an important contributor to compassion competence. We define organizational culture following scholar Edgar Schein, who wrote about it as "a pattern of shared basic assumptions learned by a group . . . which has worked well enough to be considered valid and, therefore, to be taught to new members as the correct way to perceive, think, and feel."[7] In Schein's work, culture is observable in three ways. Easiest to see are symbols and artifacts, like a building and how it is decorated; harder to see are values; and hardest to see are basic assumptions that become taken for granted about "the way things are around here."

Two aspects of organizational culture are particularly important in understanding compassion competence. First, organizational cultures teach members basic assumptions about human nature and human relationships. When cultures teach their members that humans by nature are essentially good, capable, and worthy of compassion—what we called the positive default assumption in chapter 4—these cultures enable more generous interpretations of suffering and legitimize compassionate action. We sometimes refer to the bundle of assumptions that enable compassion in an organizational culture as an organization's emphasis on shared humanity. We saw the importance of *shared humanity* in chapter 4 as well. The assumption that in an organization we all belong to one human family speeds and eases patterns of compassion by enabling us to take for granted the idea that others are capable, worthwhile, and acting with good intentions.

A second aspect of culture that is important for compassion competence involves what Edgar Schein calls *espoused values*, an organization's stated and lived-out ideals, goals, and aspirations. Values that emphasize human worth and human interconnection enable compassion competence. These are often stated in words like *dignity, inclusion, respect, teamwork, collaboration, partnership, support, care, kindness, stewardship, service, justice,* and *fairness.* Values such as these support patterns of compassion by working in the background when suffering surfaces to guide people's attention about what is important in a response. Humanistic values in organizations color interpretations of suffering as worthy of compassion and fuel competence.[8]

Organizational scholars Sigal Barsade and Mandy O'Neill have investigated organizations that manifest what they term cultures of "companionate love" that are characterized by values such as affection, care, and respect. These cultures reinforce basic assumptions about shared humanity and worthiness, featuring values that set the stage for compassion. Cultures of companionate love foster better results for organizations, generating higher customer and employee satisfaction and lowered costs from absenteeism, burnout, or turnover.[9] These cultures also fuel what social psychologists Jennifer Crocker and Amy Canevello refer to as "compassionate interpersonal goals."[10] Goals that emphasize collaboration, building trust and respect, and the need to work together to "win together" are also known as *ecosystem* goals. Such goals orient us to view ourselves as interdependent with others and build on the humanistic values and assumptions of shared humanity that support compassion competence.

In contrast, organizations can build cultures that assume people are lazy or untrustworthy, often adopting values that reinforce competition and setting what researchers call *egosystem* goals. In an egosystem, as it sounds, people prioritize self-promotion and self-focused gain, with goals like "make all the money I can and get ahead of other people." Values such as winning at all costs lead these cultures to disregard the losers, undermining the sense of shared humanity. Those who suffer are assumed to deserve to lose and are therefore unlikely to be imbued with the worth that supports compassion. In chapter 13, we describe the example of Enron as it built a culture of ruthlessness. The organization spawned egosystem goals, creating a system in which the top executives became very wealthy while stripping others with less power of their jobs and their life savings. An organization's culture infuses the assumptions we make about people, the values we hold, and the goals we set. When these involve getting ahead of other people, winning at all costs, and taking the spoils for ourselves, compassion fades into the background. By contrast, when a culture involves us in seeing others with dignity, working together for shared gain, and envisioning collective success, compassion comes alive.

At TechCo, people worked in a culture that emphasized shared humanity, with humanistic values and goals that supported an ecosystem perspective of mutual success. TechCo's stated values include "respect and care for each other," and goals include aspirational ideals that reinforce people's interdependence, like "win together." We see these assumptions and values guiding the behavior of Zeke's coworkers, who without hesitation began to muster organizational resources that might alleviate his and his family's suffering. We also see the assumptions and values in action when managers like Avi or leaders like Raoul and Barbara unquestioningly embraced the team's actions on behalf of Zeke and expressed belief that it was right and good to expand the pattern of compassion at TechCo.

KEY POINTS: HOW CULTURE AWAKENS COMPASSION COMPETENCE

- ∞ *Organizational culture* refers to shared basic assumptions about human nature as well as shared values espoused in the organization.

- ∞ Basic assumptions about human nature in organizations can emphasize or de-emphasize people's *shared humanity*, the positive default assumption that people are good, capable, and worthy of compassion as part of the one human family.

- ∞ Humanistic values such as teamwork, collaboration, inclusion, dignity, and justice characterize cultures that enable greater compassion competence.

- ∞ An organization's culture enables compassion competence through normalizing inquiry work and generous interpretations of suffering, drawing out empathic concern and emotional expression, and making compassionate action seem like an expected part of the work environment.

ROLES AWAKEN COMPASSION COMPETENCE

In organizations, we act and interact according to roles, which are patterns of expected behavior that go along with particular positions.[11] Roles are socially determined and recognized; they identify us within the organization because others can recognize our position. Roles provide a set of internalized expectations and scripts that others will also reinforce. Roles are different from the individuals assigned to them—we take them on, which is what we mean by the expression "wearing my work hat." Anyone given a work role such as manager, teacher, physician, or file clerk learns to wear the hat, taking on a set of expectations that encompasses both how to be and how to act. For instance, a manager is expected to be firm and clear, while a teacher is expected to be warm and dedicated.

In relation to compassion competence, we focus on a distinction between *role taking* and *role making*.[12] Both can contribute to compassion competence, but they do so in different ways. Role taking, as it sounds, refers to how we learn to take on roles. This involves how roles are described, formally designed, and communicated to newcomers. Training often conveys what a role entails to help people take it on faster or more effectively. Research validates the fact that people very quickly learn how to act and be in ways that are appropriate for social or work roles.[13] We implicitly pick up what is within our zone of responsibility, and if we violate the expectations of a new role, people in the organization will correct us, so we become more and more likely to conform to the expectations that go along with it.

Roles can be powerful for awakening compassion when they are described with compassion at their core. For instance, when people become managers, they often receive managerial training.

This training can emphasize care and responsibility for employees' and customers' well-being as part of what is expected for managers. When it does, managers—like Avi at TechCo—expand their zone of responsibilities to include compassion for employees. This kind of role design can be done for any type of work. For instance, compassion architects interested in increasing compassion competence in a large urban transportation system convened groups of bus drivers and involved them in discussions about how their role linked to the larger purpose of creating a safe and compassionate city. We have seen role descriptions and training for many types of work—from bus drivers to physicians to housekeepers—redesigned in just this way, with significant effects on awakening compassion competence.

Role making is distinct from role taking. People invent and sculpt new aspects of their roles in dynamic ways over time. People learn expectations by role taking and change those expectations by role making, in which role expectations are shifted in response to social interactions and social understandings. Jane's research with Amy Wrzesniewski uses the term *job crafting* to show how people who occupy the same role can innovate what they do. People craft new or different tasks and incorporate them into their roles. People also shift the relationships they regularly engage in as part of their work role. For instance, the hospital cleaners who participated in the first study of job crafting sometimes sculpted their roles by interacting in a caring way with patients, which enhanced their work.[14] In organizations that embrace this kind of role making in the service of compassion, people create ingenious ways to shift their roles to add to patterns of compassion.

People can also innovate their roles by changing meanings and linking their work to the broader values and purpose of the organization. Our fellow organizational researchers Donde Plowman and

Laura Madden, along with other colleagues, point out the importance of this essential link between values and roles in enhancing
compassion competence. They have found that compassion becomes widespread in a complex system "when the alleviation of
suffering is internalized as a fundamental value and behavioral norm
that agents recognize, act on, and alter their roles to include."[15] The
hospital cleaners sometimes crafted their roles in this way by defining their role as healers who contributed to the broader mission of
the hospital to help people heal. At TechCo, the human resources
leader, Barbara, told us about how she changed her role from one
that focused mostly on compensation data and spreadsheets of
employee information to one in which she was a sort of "chief compassion officer" charged with making the values of the organization
come alive and doing whatever it would take to increase compassion
throughout the global company.

KEY POINTS: HOW ROLES AWAKEN COMPASSION COMPETENCE

∞ Roles are socially defined patterns of expected behavior that
  go along with particular positions.

∞ People throughout organizations rely on role expectations
  of others to make actions more predictable. When compassion is incorporated into roles, it becomes more reliable and
  predictable.

∞ Role taking is a process of learning and internalizing the
  expected patterns that go along with a position. Formal
  training and descriptions that emphasize compassion make
  it seem like an expected part of work.

∞ Role making is a process of innovating by crafting new tasks,
  relationships, and meanings into the expectations. Role
  making can enable compassion competence when people
  craft work to include more emphasis on others' well-being.

ROUTINES AWAKEN COMPASSION COMPETENCE

Organizational routines are the recurrent, interdependent ways that people accomplish work tasks.[16] We are used to participating in routines for many tasks at work, particularly hiring, tracking projects, accounting for money and time, planning for the use of resources, getting together to discuss work, making decisions, and resolving conflicts. Often compared to the ruts in a road, routines make action faster and easier to coordinate.

Two aspects of routines are crucial for creating compassion competence. First, because routines create expectations for how things happen in organizations, people don't have to think about them. They just seem like "standard practice" and happen easily. At TechCo, we saw this aspect of routines as standard practice when Avi used the TechCo communication routines to communicate Zeke's hospitalization to a broad network of executives in the organization. Because this notification was routine, Avi didn't have to debate about whether or not to alert others, and when Raoul received the alert, he did not raise questions about using organizational resources or communication channels to respond to suffering. The whole pattern was part of what had become a standard operating procedure at TechCo.

A second aspect of routines that is crucial for creating compassion competence points to the fact that although routines are taken for granted, they are not static or mindless. In fact, they are flexible and help improvisational action to take shape at work. Organizational researchers show that people simultaneously hold an expectation about how the routine is supposed to happen but deviate as they need to in order to get the task accomplished, without seeing this as a violation of the routine itself. An easy way to see this is to look at hiring routines that guide how new members are identified and brought into the workplace. Employees in the organization know how the hiring routine works, and they coordinate across many people to take the steps necessary to get approval for a new job, post a job, receive and examine applications, and select people to interview. All of these steps are relatively invisible to the interview candidate, who comes into the coordinated effort with expectations for what will happen but also can adjust to whatever is necessary to make the selection process work.

Chris Murchison, former vice president of staff development and culture at HopeLab, a Silicon Valley think tank devoted to "combining science and design to help people thrive," was masterful at weaving compassion into the organization's hiring routines. He shared a story that illustrates this flexibility in routines and how it can be used in the service of alleviating suffering. "Today at work we interviewed a job candidate, Nadia, who was particularly nervous. I decided to ask her about it, and what unfolded was an authentic conversation about the peculiarity of interviews. Now beyond the script, she soared with a new energy and stories and laughter." Because Chris was sensitive to the surfacing of anxiety and stress as a form of suffering, he was able to respond with compassion and shift the way that he and Nadia and others engaged in the hiring routine. Instead of questions about her background or past, they discussed interview expectations. This move from performing the hiring routine as a stilted interaction to performing it as an authentic conversation evoked empathy and improvised compassionate action. The hiring routine at HopeLab created conditions such that even those who did not get a job offer often "fell in love" with the organization through this relational resonance and became supporters.[17] For Chris, his actions reflected his desire to awaken compassion in the organization, regardless of whether or not someone got the job.

At TechCo we also see the flexibility of routines contributing greatly to compassion competence. The human resources group used their routines for providing insurance coverage to employees, but improvised on them to find new ways to extend Zeke's coverage, adding breadth to the resources that TechCo mobilized. The organization had developed a routine for paying out vacation-time donations to employees who needed financial assistance, and they launched this routine to help alleviate Zeke's suffering. As Zeke's expenses mounted, however, and this wasn't enough to help him receive the treatments he needed, the organization improvised on this routine by coupling it with matching grants from Raoul's division budget and from TechCo's headquarter's budget.

Thinking about organizational routines tends to be one of the most unexpected aspects of social architectures that awaken compassion. While it might seem odd to think about compassion and budgeting routines, for example, our research shows that routines put into the service of creating patterns of compassion weave a new tapestry. Organizations that deploy routines in this way are "knotted together" in ways that enhance compassion competence.[18]

KEY POINTS: HOW ROUTINES AWAKEN COMPASSION COMPETENCE

∞ Routines are defined as recognizable, recurring ways that interdependent tasks are accomplished in organizations. They provide "grooves" that guide how work gets done.

∞ People hold a view of how a routine should work, so when routines incorporate compassionate actions, the system becomes fast and reliable, and patterns of compassion are created easily.

∞ People simultaneously hold a view of what commonly happens and what needs to happen right now in order to accomplish a task. They incorporate this simultaneous view

into a routine, which makes compassionate actions easier
because they can be both standard and improvised.

∞ Many kinds of work routines can incorporate compassion,
including hiring, onboarding, offboarding, accounting, planning, meeting, communicating, budgeting, decision-making,
conflict resolution, and recognizing people.

STORIES AND LEADERS AWAKEN COMPASSION COMPETENCE

In addition to being systems of network ties, cultural assumptions and values, roles, and routines, organizations are systems of
meaning—collections of symbols, stories, and information that
come to be interpreted in shared ways as members interact with
one another and with the system.[19] In relation to compassion
competence, we point to the crucial importance of both stories
and leaders as focal points in shaping meaning in organizations.

According to scholars and management consultants alike, stories
are one of the most important ways that people share knowledge,
motivate themselves and others, build trust, convey and understand
values, and share a vision of the future.[20] Stories about the organization and about what happens in it are a primary way that members
come to share interpretations and understandings of three central
questions: what kind of place is this to work, what kind of people
are these, and what kind of person can I be while I am working here?
In our research, when people heard and shared stories of compassion at work, they came to understand the whole organization as a
more compassionate place, to see their colleagues as more compassionate people, and to realize that they could be compassionate
at work.[21] These patterns of meaning in the system make it more
likely that when suffering surfaces, members of the organization will

interpret it generously. Research by CompassionLab member Sally Maitlis demonstrates that teams can use narratives of care to engage in performance improvement and to enhance their connections; in other words, the stories that teams tell themselves can make them more or less competent in extending compassion to one another.[22] As we saw at TechCo, where stories of compassion were plentiful, while Zeke's accident happened on personal time away from his workplace, his coworkers interpreted his suffering as meaningful and relevant to them. They interpreted their organization as the kind of place that would want to respond with compassion, and these meanings of their team and their organization supported their immediate action.

Our study of how an organization responded to three of its members who lost all of their belongings in a fire showed how stories fuel compassion competence. When organizational members learned of the fire, stories about the loss spread rapidly. People started contributing funds quickly in a donation box that had been placed in the central café. Stories about how much money had been raised in a short time also began to circulate. These stories reinforced people's sense that their workplace was compassionate, and they sped up the generation of resources and amplified the magnitude of further donations, so that the organization raised more money faster. Stories that spread about compassion also sparked other ideas for resources that might be useful and generated a greater scope of resources that were more customized.

Leaders are also important focal points in systems of meaning. Members of the organization look to them for guidance about how to interpret what is happening and how to make sense of the world.[23] Members also follow models set by leaders, so a leader's compassionate actions can spur many other acts of compassion. We do not mean to suggest that compassion must be driven from the top down in organizations, however. In fact, because compassion is an emergent pattern, it is rarely controlled in a conventional top-down manner. In his book titled *The Positive Organization,* our colleague Bob Quinn shows that learning how to provoke and trust an emergent process is one of the most challenging things for leaders .to do.[24] We encourage leaders to learn how to work with emergent processes of compassion more adeptly because we see clearly in stories like Zeke's the power of leaders to amplify participation in patterns of compassion that they do not control. Leaders like Avi, Raoul, Barbara, and the CEO played key parts in expanding participation and mobilizing resources at crucial junctures in the pattern. By modeling compassionate responses to suffering, even though the unfolding process was not under their direct control, these leaders amplified compassion. Because of its tremendous amplifying power, we will explore additional aspects of compassion and leadership in chapter 10.

KEY POINTS: HOW STORIES AND LEADERS AWAKEN COMPASSION COMPETENCE

- ∞ Organizations are systems of meaning—collections of symbols, stories, and information that come to be interpreted in shared ways by members.

- ∞ Stories are focal points in systems of meaning. Compassion stories enhance competence by building belief in compassion.

- ∞ Leaders are focal points in systems of meaning. Leaders shape meaning by modeling compassion and by communicating about it.

- ∞ Leaders' actions and stories enhance compassion competence when they mobilize additional resources and make the pattern of compassion more sustained and customized.

■ AN INVITATION TO REFLECT ON A SOCIAL ARCHITECTURE OF COMPASSION

Understanding a social architecture that supports compassion at work shows us new ways of thinking about compassion in organizations. Beyond simplistic views or overly individualized accounts, this framework offers a systemic perspective. It opens up visibility into the complex and artful work involved in creating emergent patterns of compassion. This framework offers us the possibility of many starting points for enhancing compassion competence in organizations. With these new starting points come new insights about each organization. While creating compassion competence isn't simple, seeing that it is meaningfully patterned in ways that allow compassion architects to intervene ignites a sense of grounded optimism. We can catalyze action and create change that awakens compassion competence in organizations.

How would you characterize the social architecture of your organization? Use the tools in Part Four: Blueprints for Awakening Compassion at Work to create a blueprint that will help you enhance your organization's compassion competence.

9

DESIGNING FOR COMPASSION COMPETENCE

NOW THAT WE HAVE a framework for understanding how an organization's social architecture awakens compassion competence, we can actively design organizations in ways that will enhance people's capacity to notice suffering, evoke generous interpretations, increase empathy, and amplify patterns of compassionate action. We highlight a set of design principles that have evolved from our research and inform the work of compassion architects who want to change their organizations.

Trusting in these design principles can help you to develop the courage required to step into the heart of suffering at work and try new things that will provoke your system to respond. Working with these design principles also helps awaken our curiosity, because emergent patterns rarely feature simple cause-and-effect relationships. And ultimately, using these design principles changes compassion architects themselves, evoking their skill, creativity, patience, and graceful transformation right alongside the organizations they transform.

ARCHITECTURES THAT ENHANCE ATTENTION TO SUFFERING

It may seem paradoxical at first, but organizations that are filled with compassion are also filled with pain. Once we understand the compassion process, we understand this paradox, because we see that all compassion begins with expressions of suffering. In organizations where suffering is routinely ignored, compassion is also ignored. To design architectures that create compassion competence, we have to prepare the ground for more suffering to surface.

MEET MIDWEST BILLING

When we walked into Midwest Billing, we knew we'd discovered another of what organizational scholars Gretchen Spreitzer and Scott Sonenshein have called a "positive deviant" workplace.[1] As we described with TechCo, this idea refers to an organization that deviates from the norm by being far above it on some dimension. At Midwest Billing we found a very high-performing organization that was also off the charts in terms of compassion competence.[2] This simultaneous combination of excellence in terms of measurable results and human responsiveness to suffering offers a model for design principles to enhance attention to pain and ways to alleviate it.

On our first morning at Midwest Billing, we arrived early at the secured floor of this hospital billing unit, which was located within a community health care system. We were there as organizational researchers, ready to observe the unit's work. Escorted in, we took our seats in the back of their conference room space, large enough to seat all staff members around rectangular tables. We watched as thirty employees, all women, arrived for their workday. We knew in advance that Midwest Billing was what scholars would label a "pink-collar ghetto," featuring service-sector work that offered little opportunity for advancement.[3] Jobs like these have been labeled "pink collar" because they are largely populated by women, just as in this unit. Each day these billers handled the preparation and submission of hundreds of insurance claims on behalf of the physicians and clinics. But sociological facts about the industry did not begin to describe the social architecture we discovered that morning.

One table was almost invisible under a huge pile of envelopes. Behind this mountain of paper, her head barely visible, Dorothy sat with a letter opener in her hand. She told us that the envelopes contained notifications about the status of insurance claims. The unit received hundreds of envelopes every day that had to be opened and sorted, and their contents stamped and processed. She told us that this Monday, as with many Monday mornings, was a particularly heavy mail day.

Members of the unit came into the conference room chatting, notebooks tucked under one arm and carrying mugs of coffee or tea. Each one saw Dorothy behind her mountain of envelopes, set down her things, and turned around and left the room. We watched this happen again and again. One after another, members of the unit came back with letter openers in hand, grabbed envelopes from the pile, and began to open them. No one had to be asked. The meeting kicked off and everyone continued to help Dorothy. In an utterly silent and easy choreography of lending a hand, at the end of the half-hour meeting, tidy stacks of cleanly opened envelopes sat in front of each seat. What would otherwise have been a half day of dull work was done.

We had just witnessed an organization whose members were keenly attuned to one another and practiced at paying attention and responding to the need for help. This is an important point because our research has shown that regular, consistent, normalized

help giving is a condition that supports high-quality ties and connections between people—something that we know sets the stage
for compassion competence. We quickly discovered that their attention, attunement to one another, and quick responsiveness to
one another's need for help did not stop with work tasks. They
had a wide variety of ways to help and support each other with
suffering that came in from outside the unit as well. We knew that
pink-collar work is usually also low-wage work, and this kind of
labor is statistically correlated with many kinds of suffering that
flow from sources such as poverty, divorce, and domestic violence.
When we got there, we found that a majority of the members of
Midwest Billing were single mothers striving to care for their children on modest wages. Many were also caring for an elderly family
member or other extended family members in their households,
stretching their paychecks even further. Looking at the unit through
a sociological and statistical window, we expected to see a lot of
suffering that corresponded predictably with financial and social
strain. But looking through the window of workplace community,
we saw an exquisite social architecture designed to draw attention
to these prevalent forms of suffering, offer generous interpretations
of them, increase empathy and concern, and amplify patterns of
compassionate action, all with the same kind of easy choreography
that we witnessed with Dorothy and the envelopes.

DESIGNING TO CONNECT THROUGH CARE

In network terms, Midwest Billing was a small group of people who
were strongly connected by being members of the same organizational unit. They occupied a secured space, which made the unit
physically separate from other units within the organization. This
separation further emphasized the members' sense that they were
interconnected within a special subnetwork that was different from

the larger organization. The structure of these network ties helped them feel seen and known at work. And as we saw in chapter 5, the identification that comes from doing similar work and being in a similar work environment fosters feelings of empathy and concern for each other. So our first design principle for compassion architects involves looking for ways to create subnetworks within larger organizations or systems where people can identify with each other and feel more fully and authentically known. These subnetwork structures and the feelings that flow through the ties help direct attention and empathy when suffering surfaces, and they evoke more generous interpretations and customized actions. When people do not feel that they are just a number in a large system or a cog in a big machine, we've begun to design for compassion.

Design principle

Create subnetworks within larger organizations or systems where people can identify with each other and feel more fully and authentically known.

Members of Midwest Billing emphasized the quality of connections with coworkers as a primary focus of their working lives. They built high-quality connections through trusting each other to get things done, playing together in ways that kept work positive, helping each other when things got hard, and respecting each other no matter what happened.[4] They designed recruitment and hiring routines that emphasized fit with the group as well as billing knowledge and skills. They knew that corrosive connections were deadly to the subculture they had created, and they worked to keep them from forming. These routines reinforced the value of high-quality connections at work for newcomers and longtime members alike. This informs another design principle for compassion architects:

Design principle
_____

> Revamp selection and hiring routines to emphasize high-quality connections, empathy, and fit with the cultural assumptions and values of shared humanity at work.

In several ways, Midwest Billing was more like a high-performance manufacturing unit than a billing department. The unit met every day at 8 a.m. to discuss data and make decisions about rapid performance improvements. This daily meeting also became a place for sharing relational information and surfacing suffering. One member described this dual focus supported by the routine: "The morning meetings kind of bring us all together as a whole, so we can kind of touch base that way. It's not always business oriented. We do talk business, as you know, but we also have the occasional sharing of other things if we need to. I think that keeps us informed, like a person's sick or they're having surgery or whatever—that's the time that those type of things come out." In fact, the unit regularly adjusted the collective workload based on information shared at the morning meeting about members who were sick or absent or just not feeling like themselves and in need of help. Task loads could be quickly calibrated to available help, ensuring that both empathy and effort flowed to where it was most needed. This informs our next design principle:

Design principle
_____

> Create meeting or gathering routines that bring people into regular, consistent contact with each other, and make space to discuss both work performance and relational needs for help or support.

Over time, as Midwest Billing grew and took on more demands, the unit discovered that they could increase their overall efficiency if they worked in teams rather than individually. These smaller team structures served as sub-subnetworks, connecting people even more strongly to a few coworkers, so that they worked together closely and knew each other well. During this move into a team structure, the unit also gained efficiency by centralizing some tasks that took time each day, like opening the huge stacks of mail or double-checking claim numbers. While this "shared service" model in the unit could have created suffering by making some members feel less valuable, Midwest Billing guarded against this by highlighting its core value of support and tying these jobs directly to that core value. Naming this team the "support pod" reinforced the tie to the cultural value of support that pervaded the unit.

Midwest Billing adapted its onboarding and training routines to incorporate the support pod. Any newcomer, regardless of the role she was hired to fill, began by working in the support pod for a period of time. The billing department's new team structure, combined with the core values and the routines, placed the support pod at the unit's heart. Plentiful appreciation and regularly expressed gratitude for the support pod elevated members from a role that could have been denigrated as second-class citizen to what many billers said was "the most important role here." With the support pod visibly central and valued in the unit, this web of care paid off in more ways than one.[5] Midwest Billing climbed to industry-leading results by increasing efficiency in its time to collect money. At the same time it brought its turnover to under 5 percent in an industry that regularly sees turnover rates of 50 percent or more. This amalgam of elements of the social architecture highlights our next design principle:

Design principle

Regard organizational change that improves efficiency as an opportunity to simultaneously increase compassion. In any change process, tie change to core assumptions and values of shared humanity, and redesign roles and routines to elevate people's sense of responsibility for others' well-being.

DESIGNING TO LOWER THE COST OF EMPATHY

Sociologist Candace Clark, in a broadscale examination of compassion in American life, noted that we participate in an invisible "sympathy economy," in which sympathy is seen like any other good, to be spent or saved or used depending on individual circumstances.[6] Her work echoes what we saw in chapter 5: when sympathy or empathy seems costly in terms of time, effort, or reputation, we reduce our concern and compassion correspondingly. And in organizations where receiving compassion is perceived to go along with being indebted to others, people sometimes withhold revealing suffering in an attempt to avoid this sympathy debt. Some forms of a sympathy economy can make suffering harder to see and empathy harder to feel.

The idea of a sympathy economy is useful for compassion architects, because they can also design to increase what Deborah Prentice and Dale Miller describe as the "psychological subsidies" of compassion.[7] Cultural or subcultural values of care and support, like those we see at Midwest Billing, reduce the perceived costs of empathy. Norms that foster helping on a regular basis decrease the sense of obligation or debt that comes with asking for and receiving help. Coupled with informal recognition, such as praise or appreciation, cultural assumptions and values can change the sympathy economy so that compassion becomes rewarding. This shift was evident at Midwest Billing, where one member actually described the unit in terms of an economy of care: "I think as far as getting the group to be a caring group, I think they learn by example. Caring isn't necessarily a reward for the person receiving the care; it's a reward for the person doing the caring—the feeling that you have that you've done some good and you've gone out of your way to help your fellow human. That's the reward." More formal rewards for care and support were also abundant. For instance, a stack of gold-star awards sat in the unit conference room, available to all members at any time. People wrote stories of help, support, excellent performance, and care on the back of gold stars that were shared at the daily meetings. All gold-star awards hung above the cubicles of the recipients, so a visitor walking into the unit was greeted with constellations of care and support spread across the workplace. These formal reward routines, combined with culture and informal practices, helped shift the sympathy economy dramatically toward rewarding compassion rather than undermining it.

Design principle

Emphasize informal recognition and formal social recognition of compassionate actions in line with cultural values and assumptions to shift the sympathy economy in ways that make compassion rewarding rather than costly.

Members of Midwest Billing participated in practices and routines that discouraged or punished violating their shared workplace cultural values. For example, all members maintained a strict no-gossip communication practice with each other. They would gently refuse to participate in a conversation if they perceived it as gossip. Members insisted that if someone's work or attitude was going to be the subject of a conversation, she had to be present in the conversation. They engaged in direct conversations about workplace conflicts, facilitated by coworkers or leaders, to ensure that they did not fester. These norms, practices, and routines highlight the link between courage and compassion. They also shift the sympathy economy because violating the cultural values becomes costly.

Design principle

Tip the sympathy economy toward making violations of cultural assumptions and values costly to lessen behaviors that undermine compassion.

Sarah, the manager of Midwest Billing, reinforced the cultural assumptions about shared humanity and the shared values of care and support. She modeled support by giving the unit fifteen-minute sunshine breaks at random times when the sun broke through the winter clouds, staying behind to answer the phones while everyone else went outside. She crafted her role in the unit so that concern for employees' well-being was a significant priority in her work. When difficulties or disagreements erupted, she would often emphasize a message of common humanity. She described how she would articulate this assumption: "Every employee who works with you is the same as you . . . human. There may be different levels of hierarchy within your corporation, but when all the layers are peeled back, we are all the same. So treat every one of the employees you work with as you expect to be treated."[8] These values in action inform two design principles for compassion architects:

Design principle
Coach leaders to model cultural values that support shared humanity, and model them yourself.

Design principle
Articulate the way you would state the cultural assumptions of shared humanity in your organization. Use this statement to guide how you and others engage when conflicts or disagreements erupt.

DESIGNING TO MITIGATE PERSISTENT SOURCES OF SUFFERING

One defining feature of a pink-collar ghetto, as we said, is limited opportunity for advancement or growth. As Midwest Billing continued to improve its performance and reduce its turnover rates, the lack of opportunity for career growth or advancement exacerbated suffering. Some members left the unit to pursue other forms of work. One member reduced her hours to part-time and began to work toward a nursing degree. For most members, though, additional schooling or a career change was too expensive or too taxing. Recognizing that boredom or stagnation could be a persistent source of suffering, the group began to develop a more elaborate cross-training routine, not only to help newcomers learn the ropes but also to allow billers to move across teams. This routine enhanced the opportunity for people to build new skills and began to address this form of suffering.

Looking for growth potential in the unit, Sarah asked the teams to name informal leaders. Initially, these team leaders helped by fielding questions that didn't require the manager's input. As the informal leaders became used to the new designation, they took initiative to meet as a group to build their leadership skills. They developed greater ability to facilitate dialogues about workplace conflict, which freed up Sarah's time. They took on responsibility for tracking data. Team members came to rely on the team leaders for guidance. After these roles had developed so well, Sarah approached the human resources division of the hospital system to have the team-leader positions formally recognized. She lobbied for additional compensation for their added responsibilities, which was approved. This creative approach to unit development reveals another design principle:

Design principle

Invent roles and training routines that address persistent sources of suffering in work, such as boredom or lack of opportunity for advancement.

The day when approval came for these new roles to be formally recognized and compensated, the unit held a ceremony naming each leader queen for a day, decorating them with symbolic crowns, and celebrating their success. The imaginative creation of these roles served as an antidote to the suffering that comes from stagnation and hopelessness in work environments where people perceive that they have no opportunity for growth. Celebrating this success at changing the social architecture further enhanced people's belief in the compassion of the organization and their capacity for growth and change. While it might seem modest in some ways, the fact that Midwest Billing created multiple paths for career advancement out of what started as a single-level, single-service job designation is a triumph of opportunity in the face of suffering.

Design principle

> Celebrate compassionate action regularly to strengthen relationships and reinforce people's belief in their capacity to increase compassion in the organization.

ARCHITECTURES THAT EVOKE GENEROUS INTERPRETATIONS OF SUFFERING

Organizations can make generous interpretations of suffering difficult, particularly when they involve someone's failures at work, as we saw in chapter 4. Sometimes work distracts us with time and performance pressures or focuses us on financial goals that limit our view of others' humanity. In those situations, we need a social architecture that reawakens our capacity for generous interpretations of the challenges, difficulties, and failures that cause suffering at work. How can we design workplaces that evoke these generous interpretations, especially in times of great pressure when they are most likely to break down?

DESIGNING GOALS THAT REINFORCE
COMMUNITY ASPIRATIONS

Research emphasizes that when we see ourselves as part of an inter-connected community at work, a human family or an *ecosystem*, we interpret people's plights differently than when we think we are only in it for ourselves. As we've shown, self-interested *egosystem* views lead us to interpret people's suffering as irrelevant to our own success. An egosystem pushes us toward goals that involve our own gain and ignore our impact on others. On the other hand, when we see ourselves as part of a community that succeeds or fails together, we interpret people's suffering as important and worthy of compassion. An ecosystem pushes us toward goals that involve collective gain and investment in the common good.

We see an example of ecosystem goals in the story of Julie Morath, who is now president and CEO of the California Hospital Quality Institute. When she served as the chief operating officer (COO) at Children's Hospital and Clinics of Minnesota, beginning in 1999, Julie set an impossible-to-achieve community aspirational goal of 100 percent patient safety.[9] As scholar Amy Edmondson notes in her book *Teaming*, where she describes Julie's work, this goal was years ahead of the mainstream of her field. At the time, physicians and nurses were unfamiliar with or unwilling to acknowledge the widespread harm caused by medical errors. But Julie recognized that this issue was prevalent and could be addressed only by a professional community that was willing to embrace its interdependence and use it to aspire to greater compassion.

Design principle

Set aspirational community goals that help people see that their success is tied to their interdependence in a human ecosystem where everyone is striving for compassion and common good.

This aspirational community goal mattered to Julie because she knew the harm of medical errors in an immediate way. When asked to explain why she was on a mission for 100 percent patient safety, she told the story of an event that had haunted her for thirty years. Working as a nurse at another hospital early in her career, she saw a four-year-old patient die from an anesthesia error. Julie witnessed the devastation that the child's death caused for the family. But even more devastation followed. In Julie's words, "The nurse who felt responsible went home that day and never returned, giving up the career she loved due to a profound and crushing feeling of guilt."[10] Julie described an even wider ripple of suffering that spread through the organization: "Doctors and other nurses just shut down and never talked to one another about what happened."[11] Thirty years later, Julie is still using the pain of that intense period of suffering to motivate and lead others in ways that create possibilities for more generous interpretations of failures and the suffering they engender.

Design principle

> Share stories of times when a lack of generous interpretations of errors has caused suffering in the organization to show how generous interpretations can alleviate this suffering.

To achieve this aspirational community goal, Julie worked with others to institute a routine called *blameless reporting*, based on the positive default assumption about colleagues that we discussed in chapter 4. This routine rests on the assumption that everyone in the hospital is acting on good intentions and striving for the best possible care for their patients. The routine invites examination of errors and near misses to foster learning. Even as this routine opens up more visibility about people's errors, it fuels more generous interpretations of the suffering of patients, doctors, nurses, and staff when errors occur.

People throughout the system participate in the routine and make meaning of errors in ways that engender compassion.

Design principle

Institute routines for discussing errors, failures, mistakes, and near misses in your organization in ways that foster generous interpretations of suffering to reduce blame and emphasize learning.

Julie's example shows us an amalgam of leaders' actions, stories, cultural assumptions, and routines that evoke generous interpretations of suffering at work.

DESIGNING DECISIONS THAT EVOKE GENEROUS INTERPRETATIONS OF SUFFERING

How people make decisions at work, and the frameworks that are called upon to guide those decisions, greatly shape interpretations of suffering. These can be small-scale decisions about everyday work tasks or large-scale decisions about organizational action. We saw this in our research when Richard, the CEO of a construction firm, recalled an instance of decision-making that steered him away from a generous interpretation of a traumatic safety event:

A young child climbed over a fence and was badly burned by a piece of equipment on the organization's property. Immediately, as CEO, I began to get advice. "Don't admit any wrongdoing," the attorneys told me. The investigators told me that this boy had to go over a fence to get to the equipment, and he had to pry open a door, and that's how he got hurt. And so we could have taken a legal stance that we were not at fault. But the truth of the matter is that the investigators and attorneys and other staff just got me worried about everything.

When something has gone wrong, the worry about unknown consequences and the impulse to protect the organization can blind us to suffering. Roles such as attorney, risk manager, investigator, or human resources officer can hinder compassion when they are designed to emphasize only the responsibility of protecting the organization, without an eye toward also protecting people's well-being. Compassion architects can design roles that support more generous interpretations of suffering by emphasizing that everyone in the organization has a responsibility for the well-being of the organization's stakeholders.

Design principle

Describe roles, especially roles that involve investigation or risk management, with explicit responsibility not only for protecting the organization but also for protecting the well-being of a range of stakeholders.

In Richard's case, he did not have the benefit of attorneys and investigators whose roles invested them in compassion for all stakeholders. But Richard was not just a CEO; he was also a father. When he looked at what had happened in his role as CEO, he felt "worried about everything." But when he looked at the situation in his role as a father, the decision seemed more obvious:

> I had to hold a press conference, and I had been fully prepped by my legal team. But you know what? I couldn't help but put myself in the shoes of that child's parents. I got up there in front of the press, and I said, "We take 100 percent complete accountability for this event. It's not a matter of fault, it's a matter of healing this young child and his family."

Richard adopted an alternative framework for decision-making that restored a generous interpretation of suffering. A less generous interpretation could have amplified suffering by painting a picture of the hurt child as reckless and irresponsible, engaging the family and the organization in a protracted legal dispute. Instead of shifting the blame toward the boy, Richard decided to offer compassion.

Design principle

When decisions involve responding to suffering, discuss the decision from the point of view of multiple roles within and outside the organization, and actively consider the perspectives of others who are involved to heighten empathy and evoke generous interpretations of suffering.

Richard's actions provided a model for compassion throughout the organization. In addition, they show us how leading with compassion can require courage, since not everyone in the organization agreed with his choice. Richard smiled ruefully as he concluded: "My staff told me the general counsel looked like he was going to have a cow." But all ended well for both the organization and the boy's family. And Richard's decision became a story that was shared widely in his organization, amplifying compassion in later decisions. Compassion architects can also draw on Richard's model:

Design principle

Uphold models of leading with compassion and share stories of compassionate decisions. Use them to spark discussions about how everyone's roles or routines can be recrafted to incorporate more responsibility for the well-being of others.

Richard's story makes plain that decision-making routines, whether by top leaders like Richard and his staff or by others at all levels, can be oriented around compassion. When decision-making frameworks and guidelines encourage people at work to take human costs into account, along with legal and financial concerns, these routines enable compassion competence. At times, giving consideration of suffering its due improves the organizational outcomes. Compassion scholar Ace Simpson has suggested that in order to design greater compassion competence into decision-making routines, organizations need to build metrics, data-collection measures, and information technologies that track and highlight suffering and compassion as an explicit and valued element of decision-making.[12] Imagine how much easier Richard's decision would have been if the organization's routines had included measures of suffering from accidents or calculations of the worth of preserving dignity for the boy and his family, instead of data solely about financial risk related to the accident. This highlights one more design principle:

Design principle

Develop frameworks for decision-making, including measures and data tracking that make visible the costs of suffering and the value of human dignity.

ARCHITECTURES FILLED WITH EMPATHY

Increasing empathy and concern in an organization often hinges on the capacity to draw people into dialogue and find forms of engagement that help us to see and feel each other's passions and fears. We saw in chapter 5 that personal and interpersonal skills such as perceptive engagement, attunement, listening, and mindfulness can increase empathy. Beyond these skills, social architectures can make it easier or harder to take other people's perspectives, and to feel and express concern, by how they involve us in structures and processes that reward concern and mitigate disdain.

DESIGNING DIALOGUE AND DISCERNMENT ROUTINES TO UNLOCK EMPATHY

Former Executive Vice President Bernita McTernan of Dignity Health, the fifth-largest health care system in the United States, described a values-based discernment process used by the system's top leadership team when they confront a difficult issue or complex decision. Bernita emphasized that in any major decision with significant implications, the leaders themselves can hold many different opinions about the best way forward, not to mention the variety of perspectives held by other stakeholders. In the values-based discernment process that Bernita described, leaders identify issues that would benefit from significant dialogue. The leadership team sets aside a period of three to five hours and invites as many stakeholders as possible to be present for the session. Each person is expected to come prepared to offer a point of view about the issue, telling the decision-makers at the table what they believe is important and suggesting the best course of action from their point of view. Bernita emphasized the importance of multiple perspectives that come out during this process: "Our discernment process is very formal, and it helps us. We see the pros and the cons, not just should we do this or not. And not just from a business point of view, but where are the values actually in conflict and how do we look at that?"

This process requires inquiry work and empathic listening. As Bernita said,

> I've learned one of the most important parts of the values-based discernment process is to listen and keep asking, "What's the right question?" I've been through many of these where the learning was to conclude that where we started isn't really the right question. You're interpreting, based on the shifting question, and after a couple of rounds of discussion, you hear people differently.

The formality of the process and the discussion that follows allow people to develop a better sense of perspective and concern for the values at stake in the decision. The process ends with a concluding circle in which people have a chance to restate what they now believe to be the correct course of action. Bernita said, "It's just amazing to me how, in so many cases—not all, of course—but in so many of them, we end up with a consensus on what was a deeply conflictual issue. It's a beautiful process."

Design principle

Adopt formal routines for inviting all stakeholders to participate in dialogue regarding important issues to reveal multiple perspectives and foster empathic listening that opens up different points of view.

Organizational scholars Warren Nilsson and Tana Paddock have developed a similar process, which they refer to as *inscaping*, in which members of an organization regularly engage in dialogue that draws out their experiences and feelings as part of their participation in a workplace. People attend regular meetings where they describe their own experience of work in relation to a shared value or goal. For instance, in a research-and-development or innovation organization with an outward focus on creativity in its market, employees would also have regular dialogues about whether it was safe for them to be creative and learn within the organization. Inscaping takes what seems to be an outer focus and involves people in talking about how that same focus affects them. Warren and Tana emphasize how much empathy develops from this kind of sharing:

The idea that organizations should turn inward may seem paradoxical at first. When we're trying to wrestle with the large and complex issues "out there," why would it help to dwell on the relatively small issues "in here"? Part of the

answer may be that, in the end, there is no "out there.". . .
As members of an organization speak honestly with each
other about their experiences of life and work, they come to
understand that the social realities that they seek to change
are not purely external. *They are in the room.*[13]

We've offered the insight that "there's always pain in the room,"
an insight echoed by inscaping research. For organizations that care
about creating a compassionate world, inscaping that focuses on
compassion as people experience it at work "in here" is another way
to build the capacity for compassion "out there" as well.

Design principle

Involve people in sharing their personal experiences of
compassion at work in a consistent manner as a way to
heighten empathy and reveal new ideas for enhancing
the organization's compassion competence.

DESIGNING FOR PLAYFULNESS

When we focus on creating an organization filled with empathy,
a focus on playfulness offers an unexpected but valuable source of
attunement, perceptive engagement, and empathic concern. While
many people hold a view that work is the opposite of play, this old
truism isn't actually true. When playfulness thrives as both a value
and a repeated practice in organizations, it enhances compassion
competence. At HopeLab, the Silicon Valley–based technology
think-and-do tank we mentioned earlier, the organization adopted
a core value that they referred to as "play with purpose." They tried
to infuse play and fun into almost all of their work activities. One
of their first endeavors involved developing a video game for children with cancer, in which kids playfully battled against a variety of
cancer cells. HopeLab designed the game with the participation of

the kids it was designed to serve, with the result that the customers and designers developed deep relationships with one another which heightened the empathy in the game's design. After it was launched, a scientific, randomized controlled trial that tested the effects of playing the game showed that kids experienced psychological and health benefits. The playful engagement in the game increased their sense of control over their cancer and their understanding of how their treatments worked, leading to greater adherence to their treatment protocols and better mental and physical health outcomes.

Design principle

Involve clients and customers in appropriately playful engagement with the organization or its products as a means of fostering the ability to take their perspective and increase the empathic design capacity.

HopeLab's leaders and members introduced play with purpose into their own work as well. Each year, the HopeLab staff celebrates a "Fun Day" together. In one of these Fun Day celebrations, a group of HopeLab employees envisioned the Fun Day as a metaphorical gathering around a campfire to reflect on the year. To bring the metaphor to life, the group commissioned an artist, Sheri, to build a ceramic campfire. Sheri created an art piece that, when fully assembled, represented a beautiful campfire, but it could also be disassembled so that all of the staff members could take their flame as a symbolic reminder of their contribution to HopeLab. Sheri described her experience of the HopeLab Fun Day: "There was more laughter and love in that room . . . it felt so full, really full. My face actually hurt from laughing; I just ached from laughing. It wasn't silly laughter and joking. There were tears; there was a full range of emotion. I thought it was incredibly beautiful." The HopeLab Fun Day retreats offer playful ways to engage people in what work means, to value connections, and to literally as well as metaphorically restore warmth to work.

Design principle

Host retreats or gatherings that engage people in playful interactions with symbols of compassion and explore how they relate to their work as a means of increasing empathy.

Fun, humor, and play might seem like unexpected additions to an ecology of values that support compassion competence, but playfulness has long been lauded for bringing people into relation with each other in new ways, opening up terrain for exploration, and attuning people to one another in organizations.[14] Playing helps create social architectures full of empathy because as we play together, we learn to pay attention to small cues about others' well-being at work. As one member of Midwest Billing described this, "Because we play, [we] can sense when things aren't right. Normally I'm a loud, funny-type person, but if there's a day when I'm sad or I'm not as talkative as normal, or if I'm not as receptive to funny jokes or anything, then they know that there's something going on." Like HopeLab, Midwest Billing was a brilliantly playful unit. When one group was particularly behind in work because they had taken on billing for a new clinic that had a lot of rejected claims, the entire unit threw a "claim rejection party," where they brought in snacks, decorated the office in bright colors, and all set aside their own work for a day to work on the older claims that had been rejected and needed to be resubmitted. This combination of play and work bolstered performance and added horsepower to what otherwise looked like an underperforming team. At the same time, it reinforced connections between members and generous interpretations for falling behind in a heavy workload.

Design principle

Use play as a response to workplace suffering by drawing people into imagining new ways that they could collectively respond to problems or difficulties that make participating in the response fun and engaging.

These two organizations look very different on the surface. One is highly scientific and based in a global technology capital. The other is administrative and based in a small rural community. Yet each found ways to use play as part of designing architectures filled with empathy.

ARCHITECTURES THAT AMPLIFY COMPASSIONATE ACTION

When suffering surfaces and generous interpretations speed feelings of empathy and spread calls for help, motivated people across an organization want to act with compassion. A social architecture that fails to offer routes for meaningful and coordinated action can lead to the paradoxical result that systems full of compassionate people often do nothing in the face of suffering. At its most competent, however, compassionate action is coordinated across many people, adjusted in relation to emerging needs, and generative in creating a breadth of resources that are highly customized to those who are suffering. Compassion architects need principles that help them draw out, speed up, and coordinate compassionate action across a system.

DESIGNING TO EXPAND FROM SIMPLE TO ELABORATE

When improvisational compassionate actions unfold across an organization, they often exhibit resourcefulness by beginning with whatever is easily and quickly at hand and expanding into more elaborate patterns over time. We saw this resourcefulness and acceleration in a response to the situation of Angela, one of our research participants, who had received devastating personal news just before leading an important strategic planning session. Angela and Rick had married young. They were the sort of couple who always knew they were right for each other. "We were at a college dance, and I saw her across the room," Rick recounted. "I knew right then that I wanted to marry her." Within a few years, a beloved son, Jaime, was born. Angela described the time just after Jaime's birth as one of the happiest of her life. She remembered now that Rick was often tired, but it seemed natural to be tired with busy work demands and a newborn's schedule. Then came news that changed their lives. In a routine medical screening, a doctor discovered that Rick had a genetic disorder with no cure.

Beyond coping with Rick's eroding health, each year Angela and Rick had to face what had come to seem like an unbearable burden when they took Jaime to have him tested for the disease. Angela dreaded the possibility that her son might suffer with the same lifelong debilitating illness. After the latest test, just as Angela was to lead her first major strategic planning meeting, the phone rang. When she answered, the voice that crackled back caught her breath in her chest: "Mrs. Parker, this is Dr. Pankow from the children's hospital. I'm afraid I have some bad news . . ."

Angela hung up the phone quietly and walked out of her office. By the time she reached the conference room, she felt in control and ready to run her meeting. "One foot in front of the other," she said to herself. Angela welcomed the assembled group, and the meeting moved along well. Her design for engagement was working. People felt energized, and one member of the group commented, "This is the best strategic planning meeting I think we've ever had." Unwittingly, Angela gave a little sigh when she heard that. Vivian, a colleague in a different department, was sitting close enough to

Angela to hear her sigh. Thinking she was tired, Vivian asked in front of the assembled group, "Angela, you look a little tired. I'm sure that planning this meeting was a lot of work, and you've done a great job. Maybe we should end here and pick it up later?"

Angela looked at Vivian. "Oh, it's not my job. It's not because of that." Unbidden tears streamed down Angela's cheeks. "I'm sorry. I just got a call, fifteen minutes before this meeting, that my son . . ." Angela told Jaime's story. Everyone in the meeting listened intently. When she finished, she was suddenly surrounded by words of comfort. The meeting disbanded, but the action expanded.

Design principle

Offer your presence, your willingness to listen, and a simple acknowledgment that you are with the other person in the midst of his or her pain as instantly available actions you can take anytime suffering surfaces. Patterns of compassion expand.

Some of the compassion moves we saw in chapter 6 began to appear. One member of Angela's team volunteered to check in each morning until Jaime's situation became clearer. Angela's manager helped arrange some time off. Other coworkers offered to pick up the follow-up tasks from the meeting. Those who hadn't been involved in the meeting organized a meal-delivery service for the family. Someone started an errand list to ease the burdens of keeping daily life going while seeking treatment for Jaime and created an emergent role of coordinator for all the family errands. The human resources group organized a vacation-time-donation drive to raise money for Angela and her family, just as Zeke's organization did in chapter 7. Upon learning that Angela and Rick were spending countless hours in waiting rooms, the administrative assistant for Angela's team created an emergent role of expeditor for small gifts. She created a gift basket and invited everyone to add something that was fun to do while waiting. Soon it was filled with handwritten cards of encouragement and support as well as crossword books, puzzles, novels, games, magazines, and music. The administrative assistant kept the basket replenished and expedited these small reminders that people cared. To Angela, amazed by this variety of compassionate actions that continued to evolve in relation to her family's needs, each day seemed to bring a new form of support.

Design principle

Expand patterns of compassion by drawing in more people, and encourage them to engage in compassion moves that make sense to them as well as to coordinate with others.

Design principle

Watch for, support, and reward the emergent roles that people create in elaborate patterns of compassionate action, such as buffers, monitors, coordinators, or expediters. These roles make action more predictable and expand patterns by keeping action coordinated. Recognizing the knowledge and skill involved in creating these roles makes participation in the pattern more rewarding as well.

From immediate to sustained over time, from simple to elaborately coordinated, we see that patterns of compassion can expand. Simple invitations to others to participate nudge a pattern to enlarge in ways no one can predict. In some cases, elaborate patterns of coordinated compassionate action like those offered to Angela and Zeke become a form of collective creativity and fuel organizational stories that continue to inspire members for years to come.

DESIGNING TO SUPPORT IMPROVISATION

We have described how Midwest Billing evolved a number of routines that simultaneously supported its performance and enhanced its compassion competence. More than any other routine, however, the seemingly simple and unheralded routine of the daily morning meeting was central in supporting the kind of improvisational action that is often required when suffering surfaces. You'll recall that this meeting was where we met Dorothy and watched the mountain of envelopes disappear in a choreography of helping. Lasting less than thirty minutes, the morning meeting was also normally infused with play. When a member of the unit, Kallie, was shot in an episode of domestic violence, however, the morning meeting took on a whole new character and became central in the unit's improvised compassionate action.

When the group learned of the trauma, they immediately began to organize a response. Compassion moves gathered steam as people felt their way forward together. One member offered to create an emergent role as monitor and report in on Kallie's status daily. Another member began to collect donations. Another picked up the paperwork for medical leave to make it easy for Kallie to apply once she was out of intensive care. Another started to create a unique gift that would allow everyone to write words of comfort or emotional support. Checking on Kallie's recovery and weaving together a pattern of many actions became a regular part of the daily meeting.

Design principle

> When suffering requires sustained responsiveness, use a short daily meeting or check-in as a way to ensure that improvised actions are woven together and that they continue to remain coordinated over time.

When Kallie came back to work, months later, the daily meeting became a place to coordinate about safety and improvise patterns of compassionate action in the face of threat. Kallie's first few days back entailed a lockdown of the building because of a threat from her attacker. Managers and safety officers shared information in the meeting about the safety of the entire unit. Members of Midwest Billing used the meeting to discern that Kallie needed additional security in the parking garage and improvised a new parking arrangement for her. After a scare when Kallie was approached by her attacker while walking to the bank alone, members of the unit used the daily meeting to organize a buddy system so that Kallie did not have to go anywhere alone during work time. Others were available to alert police if needed. The fact that members of the unit were practiced at meeting regularly, sharing information with each other, paying attention on a daily basis to the well-being of others, and improvising actions to help each other made it easier for them to adapt to all of these changing security needs. All the while, they kept up daily check-ins on Kallie's well-being, often just asking, "Do you need a hug today?" And they kept weaving tokens of care into Kallie's daily work life even as they coordinated to keep her, and themselves, safe. Kallie described it this way: "So we've got a buddy system for me. I never go anywhere by myself. If I'm breaking alone, or I'm lunching alone, and I need to leave the building, I tell somebody. I don't go by myself. There's a lot of people here that look out for me."

Design principle

> When suffering requires elaborate patterns of improvised action, ensure that those who are suffering are matched with a buddy or someone who can monitor their well-being and help adjust the pattern in a quick, mindful way.

The fact that Midwest Billing could improvise elaborate and constantly changing patterns of compassion in response to Kallie's circumstances is another tribute to their compassion competence. Members took pride in the fact that their unit was so capable of extending compassion at that scale. As we've said, the belief that we work in a compassionate organization is itself a resource for motivating and orchestrating compassionate action.[15] Our research has documented significant power in witnessing compassion at work, even if we do not actively participate. Elaborate patterns of coordinated compassionate action elevate us and give us a new vision of what's possible in our work.[16]

Design principle

Witnessing or participating in an elaborate pattern of compassionate actions becomes a source of pride, elevation, and motivation that expand people's views of what is possible in relation to compassion at work.

At its height, whether in TechCo or Midwest Billing or HopeLab, compassion competence inspires and elevates us. In Zeke's story, or Kallie's, or Angela's, we see the majesty of elaborate patterns of compassionate actions and how a sense of awe grows from witnessing this form of beauty and resourcefulness at work. People are called by the rhythm of this dance, finding pride and meaning in participating. While all kinds of things might distract us or derail these fragile improvised patterns, architectures that expand compassionate action make us more capable in the face of pain.

◼ AN INVITATION TO REFLECT ON DESIGNING FOR COMPASSION COMPETENCE

Looking in depth at one organization like Midwest Billing gives us a snapshot of a distinctive social architecture that draws a great deal of attention to people's state of mind and heart and offers insight into design principles that we can use to awaken compassion competence in our own organizations. There is no one silver bullet to make organizations more compassionate. That is why we must draw on a sophisticated framework and use a number of design principles. We also use our wisdom and intuition, honed by our being a compassion architect in our unique organizational circumstances. Without relying on overly simple cause-and-effect relationships, we have explored a number of design principles that help us to actively design for compassion competence. The tools in Part Four: Blueprints for Awakening Compassion at Work offer a set of strategic and practical questions that build on these design principles. Use the tools to create your own blueprint for compassion competence in your organization, so that when the call for compassion sounds, you can trust that your organization will respond.

How can you tap into the curiosity and courage involved in becoming a compassion architect?

10

LEADING FOR
COMPASSION
COMPETENCE

WE LOOK TO LEADERS FOR guidance, particularly in times of suffering, as we search for a vision of compassion. Leadership scholar Ron Heifetz points out this emotional tie between leaders and followers in the midst of adversity: "In times of distress, we turn to authority. To the breaking point, we place our hopes and frustrations upon those whose presumed knowledge, wisdom, and skill show the promise of fulfillment. Authorities serve as repositories for our worries and aspirations, holding them, if they can, in exchange for the powers we give them."[1]

We have hinted at the symbolic power of leaders to model compassion and shape meaning in an organization's social architecture, but here we explore this central role in greater depth. We have seen leaders' power to mobilize resources in stories like Zeke's. Because of the potency of leaders' instrumental and symbolic influence on patterns of compassion in organizations, we want to take a deeper look at the leader's role in awakening compassion competence.

TWO WAYS IN WHICH LEADERS AWAKEN COMPASSION COMPETENCE

Our research reveals two broad avenues by which leaders awaken compassion competence in their organizations.[2] They mirror the distinction we have made between parts 2 and 3 in this book: compassion in interactions and system-level compassion competence. The first avenue is what we will refer to as *leading with compassion*; the second we will call *leading for compassion*. Understanding the first avenue of leading with compassion involves taking seriously the symbolism of leaders and the power of their behavior as a model. Leaders guide many others throughout the organization about how to think, feel, and act when suffering surfaces, simply by how they act. Recall Sarah, the manager at Midwest Billing, whom we described in chapter 4 as leading with compassion when an employee in her unit, suffering from the sudden discovery of her husband's affair, lost control and engaged in an uncivil attack at a meeting. What we mean by leading with compassion is illustrated by the way that Sarah modeled a calm and thoughtful response to Jada's outburst as well as a generous interpretation of Jada's suffering. This model offered transformative power by virtue of creating a very visible template for how to be calm and compassionate in the midst of great pain. Theories of transformational leadership rest on the idea that leaders create change by first shifting themselves, transforming their own action so that others can emulate their model.[3]

We contrast leaders' moves that involve modeling compassion in their interactions with what we refer to as *leading for compassion*. Understanding this second dimension of leadership involves looking at how leaders use their position to shift the social architecture and direct resources that can be used to alleviate suffering. In Zeke's story at TechCo, we noted a number of leaders' actions that unlocked significant financial resources, ranging from Raoul's approval of matching funds to the CEO's reviewing the case and approving it. Actions of leaders take on influence and contribute to stories of compassion that mobilize resources. In their special position in the social architecture of organizations, leaders have an outsized impact on compassion competence.

Leading *with* compassion and leading *for* compassion are not mutually exclusive. In chapter 9 we met Richard, the CEO of a construction firm, who led *with* compassion for a boy who had been involved in an accident on a construction site. He simultaneously led *for* compassion by changing the decision-making framework used by his organization to evaluate legal risk as part of its response to suffering. Leading with and for compassion often build on one another. But these two forms of enhancing compassion competence in a system can also be decoupled. In large organizations, most people do not have interpersonal interactions with top leaders, but they still look to them for clarity about what matters. Some leaders may come across as less compassionate in daily work interactions but spearhead changes that enhance compassion competence in the system. Let's look at the different ways that leading with compassion and leading for compassion appear in the work of real leaders in many kinds of organizations.

LEADING WITH COMPASSION

In their book *Resonant Leadership*, Richard Boyatzis and Annie McKee show how effective leaders cultivate relationships that rest on truly knowing other people as full human beings, attuning to them, listening closely to their frustrations and joys, and caring about them deeply.[4] They also point out that compassion in these relationships offers a form of renewal for leaders. These connections remind people who occupy positions of great stress of the satisfaction and pleasure that come from being wholeheartedly with others. To lead with compassion requires that leaders learn and use the kinds of tools and insights we focused on in the second section of the book, weaving more attention to the full human state of others into their work relationships.

In our research at HopeLab, an organization we studied extensively and have described earlier, we found a powerful example of leading with and for compassion in the former president and CEO, Pat Christen. She commonly used her day-to-day interactions to learn about employees' lives and to respond to life struggles with compassion. She also used what she learned about suffering in the organization to invest in new initiatives, routines, and role crafting that shifted the social architecture. For instance, she led an initiative to remove all boundaries and restrictions from training funds, encouraging employees to use a pool of money to learn anything that would develop them as whole people.[5] She supported a shift from roles defined as managing "human resources" to roles focused on building a more compassionate culture. As a leader, Pat became attuned to the beauty of compassion. She felt it was important to restore people's sense of beauty and wonder as part of her leadership. In a letter she sent to HopeLab employees following a celebration of her as a leader, she epitomized what we have described as a culture of companionate love, and elevated and inspired members of the organization to continue to strive for and recognize the beauty in compassion:

> Dear HopeLab Family,
>
> This is a love letter. I wanted to be sure that I communicated to each of you what happened to me during our beautiful celebration on Friday afternoon, as it was simply impossible for me to do in the moment.

On Thursday evening, I spent several hours with a list of your names and thought about each one of you in the specific. I highlighted next to your names amazing things you have accomplished at HopeLab. When I got to the party, I was delighted to see many members of our extended HopeLab tribe as well and I stepped back inside to add their names to my list. It was easy enough to do. Everyone present has much to be celebrated in the "accomplishments" category.

In the end, what I penned is quite a beautiful list and a wonderful testament to your commitment to our mission and purpose. I had intended to draw upon it during my remarks. However, when I got up to speak, several things happened to me at once.

First, I was awash in memories.

Second, when I turned to look at each one of you, table-by-table, I was swamped with memories, not of your accomplishments, but even more significantly of times when we struggled as individuals, as teams, in community. This new "list" being written in my mind in real time as I scanned each of your precious faces was far more powerful, poignant, intimate, and important than the "accomplishments" list.

That is the list that demonstrates our deepest commitment to ourselves and to community. This struggle to persevere in the face of deep challenge and adversity is not always pretty. We are a mess at times as we navigate our shortcomings, our losses, and those places where we do not live up to our highest aspirations. But what I want you to know is that I was simply overcome by and in awe of what you have done—each of you—to persevere, to be better, to try again, to pick yourselves up, to wade

back into the fray, to not give up on yourselves,
on one another, on our work, on our community,
on our world. This is how we nurture deep
connection and stay on purpose together. There
is an abiding, unimaginable power in this, in *you*.
Don't ever forget that.

When leaders like Pat lead with compassion, attention to each
other more easily grows into attunement. Our circles of concern widen
into love. Generosity grows for the suffering that may sometimes make
work life messy and difficult. Leading with compassion restores our
belief in a better future so that we can feel our way forward together.

INTERPERSONAL AND EMOTIONAL SKILLS IN LEADING WITH COMPASSION

We have also mentioned Chris Murchison, a former vice president
of staff development and culture at HopeLab. Chris is another example of an attuned leader and compassion architect who uses his
attention, empathic listening, and inquiry work to draw out generous interpretations of suffering. Chris told us a story that illustrates
the skills involved in leading with compassion:

A colleague asked me if I had a minute. I've learned that
requests that start with this question are rarely a minute in
length! Davin was relatively new to our organization and
was full of worry that he was not meeting expectations
in his performance or that he was somehow missing the
mark. I listened carefully and asked questions to illuminate
specifically where and how he believed he was failing. My
questions actually shed light *not* on any shortcomings that
Davin was exhibiting in his work, but rather on some internal standards for himself that were extraordinarily high. He
was, in fact, not failing at all. He was caught in the grasp

of perfectionism that, once exposed, released its grip. Our conversation allowed him to breathe and see that he was doing just fine. He was in new territory, learning at his edge. He was right where he needed to be.

Leading with compassion, Chris used his attention to surface Davin's suffering, which might have otherwise been buried in a performance-oriented conversation. Alert to the surfacing of suffering, Chris engaged in inquiry work that further illuminated what was happening, allowing both Davin and himself to develop a more generous interpretation of Davin's perceived failures. Chris's attunement and empathic listening skills opened space for a transformative conversation that shifted painful self-criticism and blame into learning and compassion.

Tough and demanding leaders who need high-quality work can sometimes forget to remain attuned to the suffering that comes from internalized standards that are out of reach. Richard Boyatzis and Annie McKee teach leaders to coach people for development, engaging them not in solving work problems but in being more fully present to the people behind the tasks.[6] We said before that leaders can both create suffering—by asking for a lot and expecting impressive outcomes—and can alleviate it—by remaining attentive to suffering and responding with compassion. Leading with compassion takes effort, though. Psychologist Susan Fiske and others have designed a number of studies that demonstrate that people who occupy more powerful positions or higher-status roles pay less attention to the nuances of people around them, relying more on stereotypes than on distinctive information.[7] In addition, leadership comes with significant stress and pressures that may psychologically lessen leaders' attention to the full humanity of others.[8] The surprising learning for many leaders is to discover the renewing power of leading with compassion.

TAKING COMPASSION FROM WORK TO HOME

Bob Chapman, CEO of engineering firm Barry-Wehmiller, has transformed his once-dying family business into a global engineering leader. Leadership writer Simon Sinek says, "If you ask Bob what his company does, he will tell you, 'We build great people who do extraordinary things.' If you ask him how he measures his results, he will tell you, 'We measure success by the way we touch the lives of people.' It all sounds rather fluffy and mushy. But for the fact that he means it—and it works."[9] Bob transformed Barry-Wehmiller through an insistence on leading with compassion. Together with scholar Raj Sisodia, Bob describes this transformation in his book *Everybody Matters*, telling the story of how he came to understand the urgent need for and value of leading with compassion both for himself and for leaders across his organization.

As Bob describes it there, "I was stunned—and as a business leader, ashamed—to see the data . . . in the United States, an estimated 88 percent of the workforce, 130 million people, go home every day feeling that they work for an organization that doesn't listen or care about them."[10] As he worked to turn the failing company around, Bob recognized that he needed to combat this widespread pain at work. He and other leaders adopted a core value of stewardship as part of a compassionate response to this form of workplace suffering. As Bob describes it, "To us, stewardship means to truly care, to feel a deep sense of responsibility for the lives we touch through our leadership. Those lives can often appear broken, as people suffer through toxic cultures and abusive leadership. Our aspiration is to heal this brokenness and restore people to their full and joyful humanity."[11]

Along with living out this core value of stewardship, Bob and his leadership team have led the company toward having more fun, which, as we saw in chapter 9, is a core aspect of cultivating an ecology of values that enhance compassion competence. These leaders work daily to personally recognize people more fully and celebrate them more joyfully as part of leading with compassion.

Bob is most moved by seeing how leading with compassion has affected people at Barry-Wehmiller in ways that go beyond work. He describes a spillover of compassion between work and home as he tells a story about how leaders in the organization check on the status of major change efforts. In this case, the organization was pursuing process-improvement changes and had seen significant results. Bob and the firm's top leaders asked three members of the change team to talk about their results—unrehearsed—in front of the company presidents and the board of directors. "When they were finished," Bob says, "I asked Steve Barlament, a manufacturing team member whom I'd never met before, a question that came to me out of the blue: 'Steve, how did it affect your life?' Without missing a beat, he said something that was transformative for me personally and for our whole cultural journey. He said, 'My wife now talks to me more.'"[12] The communication skills that Steve had developed as part of this change team, along with the learning that flows from everyday modeling of compassion, allowed him to be a better spouse. Bob encapsulates this significant and perhaps startling result that leading with compassion in organizations can create better societies as well: "This is how we can start to heal our brokenness: sending people home as better spouses, parents, children, friends, and citizens of their communities."[13] Barry-Wehmiller has become a vessel for taking compassion from work to home.

KEY POINTS: SKILLS INVOLVED IN LEADING WITH COMPASSION

∞ Leading with compassion entails using a leader's interpersonal skills to alleviate suffering in work interactions with followers.

∞ Leading with compassion becomes a powerful form of modeling compassion.

∞ Leaders can build skill in allowing suffering to surface, engaging in sensitive inquiry work, remaining mindful, attuning to others, and listening with empathy.

∞ Seeing compassion modeled in everyday work interactions opens up the possibility that an organization's members can take compassion from work to home, improving their family and community relationships.

LEADING FOR COMPASSION

In large organizations or workplaces that are globally distributed, many members never meet the leaders. These leaders may or may not lead with compassion as part of daily work interactions, but since they do not interact with most members of the organization, direct modeling of compassion is limited. That's why savvy leaders who care about awakening compassion competence in their organizations also understand how to lead *for* compassion.

COMMUNICATING THAT WE ARE ALL IN IT TOGETHER

Jeff Weiner, CEO of LinkedIn, has been a public advocate for compassion and business. Jeff published an essay titled *Managing Compassionately* on the LinkedIn platform, using the power of social media to reach LinkedIn employees and compassion architects worldwide.[14] Jeff wrote:

Of all the management principles I have adopted over the years, either through direct experience or learning from others, there is one I aspire to live by more than any other. I say "aspire" because as much as I'd like to do it consistently and without fail, given the natural ebb and flow of day-to-day operations and challenges, and the subsequent range of responses that follow, I find this particular principle harder to practice consistently than others. That principle is managing compassionately.

Let's look at two important points about communicating to lead for compassion. First, this leader is strongly and clearly articulating compassion as a cultural value at LinkedIn. Emphasizing this value as part of the culture paves the way for others to put it into action as well, as we saw in the design principles in chapter 9.

Second, Jeff personalized the value of managing compassionately by sharing his difficulties in living up to his aspirations to practice it consistently. In terms of leading for compassion, this way of communicating reinforces the assumption of people's common humanity. In essence, Jeff is saying that we all try, we all fail, and we are all in it together. This communication reinforces the assumption that everyone at LinkedIn is trying to manage compassionately, even if they don't always succeed. Such assumptions, as we saw earlier, foster generous interpretations of failures and help us give people the benefit of the doubt.

So while he cannot be physically present with employees spread across thirty countries, Jeff is leading for compassion everywhere that LinkedIn operates. Using the LinkedIn stage to communicate cultural assumptions and values that support shared humanity changes the social architecture of the organization. Since this initial publication, Jeff has continued to speak at large conferences and public events about the value of compassionate management. Journalists and others have written about the value and asked him to describe how he practices it in his own work. These public communications inspire compassion architects throughout the organization to try new things that enhance compassion competence.

INVESTING IN COMPASSION COMPETENCE

In their book *Conscious Capitalism*, John Mackey, CEO of Whole Foods Market, and scholar Raj Sisodia explore four tenets for building businesses that create value in society through ethical exchange and elevate the nobility of work. The third tenet of conscious capitalism involves what they call "conscious leadership." Resonant with our view of compassion architects, they claim, "Leadership is mostly about change and transformation. . . . Leaders are the high-level architects, builders, and remodelers of the system. . . . Leaders have an inherent systemic sensitivity that enables them to understand both how a group of people will behave as a system and how to change the system in order to change its behavior."[15] Leading for compassion involves honing this systemic sensitivity to become a high-level compassion architect. We met an extraordinary high-level compassion architect, Fred Keller, in our research.

"When I think of compassion and the workplace, I'm not sure there's a day that goes by that I don't think about it," said this founder and retired CEO of Cascade Engineering. "Almost consciously," he added with a grin of humility. Fred is an example of a leader who spent a career leading for compassion, but not by drawing attention to himself. Cascade Engineering, a leader in large-scale plastic injection molding, is a global company with sixteen hundred employees distributed across fourteen facilities. It is one of the largest certified B Corporations in the world, nationally recognized for its sustainable business practices. Cascade is dedicated to managing a "triple bottom line" that measures not only financial results, but also the organization's social impact on people and communities and its environmental impacts through its processes and products.

At Cascade, however, "we don't talk about it in compassion terms," Fred explained. "Compassion is something to be demonstrated. Talking about compassion is quite different than practicing it." Fred and other Cascade leaders have become practiced compassion architects. They shifted the way that people are interconnected with one another in the organization's networks, the way that roles are designed, and the way that routines such as hiring, decision-making, problem-solving, rewarding, and planning are done, all with an eye toward investing in compassion competence. While they have done this in many areas, one that stands out is what they refer to as their "welfare-to-career track" at Cascade. Fred and other leaders at Cascade engaged in a series of corporate experiments to establish this track. Many experiments failed, and they spent more than ten years shifting the social architecture toward greater compassion for those coming into the workforce from great poverty.

First, they provided a van service between the company's site and a local homeless shelter, hiring eight people who tried their hand at working at Cascade. Some decided not to continue working, and others exhibited work habits that were not up to the needed standards. Next, Cascade partnered with another business and offered low-wage workers a chance to progress to jobs in the higher-paying manufacturing sector. Learning that they needed even more transformative change to be successful, Fred and others changed the training routines at Cascade to involve a poverty simulation. Members of the organization virtually perform the life tasks required to hold a job and successfully navigate the obstacles facing people in poverty. A Cascade director, one of the original group who completed the training, told us that it was the most life-changing training event she had ever experienced.

I'm a pretty successful, together kind of person. And I got through that week thinking to myself, "This wasn't so bad." But when I got my simulation results back and we went through the debrief, I learned that I'd forgotten to feed my children! I'd been so focused on paying for the bus and getting places on time and all the rest. I kept my job, but I didn't feed my children. Totally forgot it. Can you imagine? I think I used to have the sense that people who were poor were lazy. But I will never again underestimate what people are going through. After that, I know that people in poverty are usually working far harder than I am.

The new training routines supported shifts in attention to suffering, more generous interpretations of the difficulties that people faced, and heightened empathy. Cascade made more changes to the organization's social architecture as the program evolved. Fred and the Cascade leaders realized that a successful program would require expanded employee support routines and new roles. They partnered with other organizations and invented new routines to help with transportation and child care. They invented a new role when the state of Michigan offered a social worker to be on-site and Cascade integrated her into a new team that provided case-management services on the job site to enable people to keep working even as they handled life demands outside of work. They changed the networks by creating smaller integration teams to help current Cascade employees and welfare-to-career newcomers to identify with each other. Cascade tied this program into its larger culture, linking it explicitly to its already-strong philosophy of a "triple bottom line." Cascade now runs a successful welfare-to-career program with a turnover rate of 3 percent or less per month, alleviating significant financial suffering in the community through these adaptations in the social architecture of the organization.[16]

LEGITIMIZING SUFFERING AND COMPASSION

Leaders are important sources of legitimacy in organizations. They help determine what is accepted and taken to be genuine and valid. Leaders who are compassion architects can enhance the competence of their organizations by legitimizing forms of suffering and responsiveness to suffering that might otherwise be silenced.[17] Our research uncovered a compelling example of how a leader can legitimize sources of suffering that may otherwise be stigmatized or silenced, and how this legitimizing process can enhance compassion competence in a system. The following is an excerpt of a letter written by the former president of Western Washington University, Bruce Shepard. He sent the letter to all students, faculty, and staff the week following a suicide on campus. Pay particular attention to how the communication legitimizes generous interpretations of stigmatized suffering and invites people to contribute to an expanding pattern of compassionate response to suicide on campus:

> Members of our community:
>
> You likely heard that, last weekend, we lost a student, a young man who tragically took his own life. Today, you saw an alert message advising that you avoid a certain area south of campus because of police activity. That incident centered on a threatened suicide. Although the distressed person happened not to be a student and no injuries resulted, I feel compelled to share several thoughts. And, several commitments for you to consider.
>
> Suicide is not easy for many of us to talk about. You may not want to even read further. I ask that you do, for the well-being of us all.
>
> As uncomfortable as the topic may be, it is truly amazing how many of our lives have been or will

be touched by suicide and the mental distress and disease that underlies it: family, friends. . . . Suicide is endemic among those in the typical college-age group. Less so among those in college than those of similar age who are not, but still, we feel this pain year in and year out.

Can we change that?

My life has been affected, having lost a college-age son to this epidemic. Our reluctance to talk about such topics—suicide, depression, other mental distress and disease—was, I concluded, part of what can make ailments like depression the deadly diseases that they can be. Because of the stigma surrounding such topics, people do not bring the manifestations of a usually VERY treatable problem to the attention of others. In my layman's view, our brains are very powerful, and mental ailments can use that awesome brainpower, reinforced by fear of stigmas, to hide their very existence from the person with the ailment. Dire consequences can then result.

So, I took a vow, no matter how personally painful it was, to never be too embarrassed or afraid to talk about these subjects. Or, about my son.

That is step one, and I encourage you to consider joining me in that vow: break the stigma surrounding these topics by being willing to discuss them just as you would any other ailment to which we beautifully complex human beings are sometimes vulnerable.

Step two is to reinforce a culture in which we take care of each other. Do pay attention, no matter how remote the possibility may be, to signs you think indicate that a person you know might do harm

to themselves. Or, to others. We take care of each
other because we care about each other.

Step three logically follows: If you see a friend or
associate manifesting problems, certainly speak to
them if you are comfortable so doing. But, don't
stop there: alert those trained on our campus to
provide help. Give the alert, share what you are
comfortable sharing, and you may do so knowing
that professionals will confidentially and sensitively
proceed.

We cannot be 100% successful, so another step is,
again, about taking care of ourselves when tragedy
does strike: to feel and share our grief and our loss
as we are today over last weekend's loss. Partly, I
believe, we help each other grieve by acknowledging
that we are changed, our lives altered by tragedy,
and it is foolish to expect to simply "get over it."

President Shepard imbues those suffering from depression or
anxiety with dignity. He reminds us that we all share brains that
are susceptible to such ailments, reinforcing our shared humanity.
The warm, inclusive tone in the letter reminds people that they
work in an organization that values taking care of each other. The
self-revelation in the letter adds to the legitimizing of suicide, as
the leader understands the stigma of this suffering firsthand. The
call to action in President Shepard's communication is designed to
draw people into an expanding pattern of noticing signs of suicide,
interpreting the suffering more generously, feeling empathy rather
than a desire to turn away, and taking action to address this form
of suffering in the organization. By drawing attention to our fellow
"beautifully complex human beings," President Shepard imbues the
whole organizational community with the kind of beauty that renews our wonder at compassion and inspires us to do more.

KEY POINTS: SKILLS INVOLVED IN LEADING FOR COMPASSION

∞ Leading for compassion involves becoming a high-level compassion architect.

∞ Leading for compassion often entails using communication channels to reach a broad audience and reinforce a culture of shared humanity.

∞ Leading for compassion can entail transformation and change of all elements of the organization's social architecture.

∞ Leading for compassion involves legitimizing suffering and compassion in the organization and drawing attention to the beauty of compassion in human communities.

∞ Leading for compassion evokes emergent patterns of compassion that expand far beyond a centralized approach.

LEADING WITH AND FOR COMPASSION IN CRISIS

It is common wisdom that we learn what leaders and organizations really value when pressure and unpredictability collide. In crisis situations, leaders, like all humans, tend to fall back on the patterns and actions that they have used in the past. This is why we emphasize the value of learning to lead with compassion in everyday interactions and everyday business issues as preparation for times of crisis or tragedy. Because of the importance of compassion in the wake of traumas and tragedies, we want to conclude this chapter with an example that illustrates how leading with and for compassion in the midst of crisis awakens compassion competence.

On the morning of September 11, 2001, Phil Lynch, president of Reuters America, was attending a meeting at the headquarters of Compaq Computer when someone burst into the conference room to tell the gathered executives that planes had flown into the World Trade Center. Phil literally ran from the meeting to the Reuters building at 3 Times Square. When he arrived, he watched with others in disbelief as the World Trade Center towers burned.[18]

Recognizing the extent of the crisis, Phil established a command center in the boardroom on the 22nd floor of the building. In the command center, Phil and his team opened a direct line with the CEO of Reuters Group and other top management team members in London. While pandemonium reigned for the first few hours as everyone attempted to get more information about what was happening, the message that the leaders conveyed to employees from the onset of the crisis was: "People first, then customers, then the business." Leaders from across the organization worked in the command center to find and ensure the safety of all Reuters staff, because Reuters had a data center in the World Trade Center and employees all around the city and all around the world. As the work to find Reuters employees proceeded, others took on the task of learning about the condition of Reuters's clients.

These improvisational actions were not the result of a plan. As a member of Reuters commented about that day, "No one has a plan for what to do when the world falls apart." Phil and other Reuters leaders had to find ways to lead with and for compassion as conditions changed hour by hour. Phil established an hourly report to employees, conveying the status of public transit and relaying information about what was happening in the city. He encouraged them to stay in the building and not to try to go home until it was safe to do so, making sure that Reuters was monitoring public transit on an hourly basis. The leaders opened the cafeteria to all, offering free food, as they made plans to house people overnight if necessary. Many senior managers did not leave the building for days.

By the evening of September 11, the organization had located all but twenty employees. Phil Lynch personally made phone calls to the homes of the twenty missing employees, leading with compassion as he explained what Reuters was doing to find everyone. By the next morning, it had become clear that two employees, who were attending a risk-management conference at the top of the World Trade Center, were still missing and had likely died in the attack. The leaders of Reuters responded immediately to what the families of the missing wanted and needed, flying them to New York, personally meeting them at the airport to shield them from the army of reporters, and providing them a car and a personal driver who used his knowledge of the city to navigate through the maze of hospitals and locations for families with missing members.

Within two days, the London office had helped the inundated employee communications staff in the United States to set up an internal website with updates about the US office, customers, and answers to frequently asked questions. This internal global communication portal helped employees worldwide to understand what responses were being carried out, what was going on with their customers and products, and what they could do to help from afar. One longtime employee commented on the care that came as Phil and others led for compassion by shaping these communication routines: "The communication flow was constant from above. You knew Phil Lynch cared. You knew they wanted the best for us. Every which way—no matter where you turned, whether it was the daily briefing, the emergency website, or walking down the hall, you just knew that everyone was out for the welfare of the employees and their safety. The message was just consistent and very compassionate."[19]

The mother of one of the employees who died in the attack came to Reuters's headquarters and asked to meet with Phil Lynch. Sharon, a member of the human resources team, described the meeting:

She refused to believe that anything had happened. This was understandable. Reuters did everything they could to help her with this. Phil Lynch called her in the mornings to make sure she had eaten breakfast. We got her a car to take her around New York. We got her sandwiches to keep her fed on visits to the hospitals. She shared stories of her son. We were very conscious that we would not challenge what she thought. . . . We kept saying we will do everything we can, and we did.[20]

One employee, witnessing this effort, commented on how the system took on new meaning by virtue of these efforts to lead with and for compassion: "I knew Reuters was a wonderful machine, but now I know it is a wonderful machine with a great big heart in the middle."[21]

To lead for compassion when tragedy strikes requires that leaders activate the networks within the organization to involve many people in the response. Phil and his team activated networks such as technical teams and global communications teams that were already primed with trust and credibility. Leading for compassion also means emphasizing and building on values of shared humanity in the culture, which Phil and his team did by emphasizing that the response was about people first, then the business. Leading for compassion also meant creating new roles on the spot, such as bringing in grief counselors and trauma specialists to be available to any employee who needed support, as well as incorporating compassion into the roles of human resources leaders and others who interacted with the families of employees who were missing. Leading for compassion in crisis also requires modified routines, such as the command center and the constant communication, that allow people to understand what is happening and mobilize resources that may be helpful in alleviating suffering as the crisis unfolds.

As the immediacy of the crisis subsided, Phil Lynch also stepped back and reflected on the broader purpose of Reuters. He ran an all-employee town hall meeting in late September to allow people to come together, tell their own stories, and reflect on Reuters's response to the events. At the meeting, Phil began by showing a picture taken by Reuters employee Shannon Stapleton and published by Reuters, a picture that captured the beloved chaplain of the New York City Fire Department, Father Mychal Judge, being carried away from Ground Zero by his colleagues. Phil read a letter from the family of Father Mychal that described how grateful they were for the memory preserved in the picture. Phil used the story to affirm the importance of the work of Reuters as a global information provider and to reinforce the idea that its work is a service to people of the world. A manager who attended the meeting described the impact of this story: "You sometimes forget what our company does. Through these events people saw what Reuters does. . . . It reminded them what was important about what we do, rather than it just being about kind of hawking an information product to a customer. That, I think, made a lot of people feel very good about working for the company."[22] Phil Lynch, leading for compassion in the midst of crisis, harnessed the power of images, stories, and rituals to carry meaning and spread emotion throughout the organization in ways that amplified the compassion competence of the system.

One Reuters employee commented on the transformative power of what it was like to watch someone lead this way up close: "Watching Phil Lynch get so involved with the families—so quickly—with their personal lives, bringing them in, comforting them, involved with their personal pain—I saw the heart—not just the company, not just technology and lines—I saw the heart of the company in him responding to the families."[23] This story highlights the fact that leaders amplify compassion competence throughout their organizations when they themselves remain present with suffering and retain the interpersonal skills required to engage suffering with compassion, even in the midst of a crisis. To lead with compassion in a crisis offers a form of beauty in the wake of tragedy that is stunning to behold. Leading this way turns us away from hardheartedness and awakens possibilities for compassion competence simply by offering a model for being human together.

AN INVITATION TO REFLECT ON LEADING FOR AND WITH COMPASSION

To lead for and with compassion isn't simple. It requires interpersonal skills and understanding of compassion as a human process coupled with organizational understanding and systemic sensitivities. Leaders are the high-level architects of compassion in their organizations. They move people by modeling personal presence in the face of suffering. They foster compassion throughout the system by their capacity to attune to others, feel concern, listen, and act with care. Leading with compassion takes on even more power when it is combined with a system-level view of leading for compassion. Leaders who invest in compassion competence and communicate to reinforce shared humanity unlock resources to alleviate suffering that they themselves may never have dreamed possible. By legitimizing suffering and compassion, leaders shape the contours of our collective empathy and offer us new ways to make more generous interpretations of one another. The examples of many leaders who remind us of the beauty of compassion open up a new window into the possibilities of creating extraordinary compassion competence.

When has a leader moved you with the wonder and beauty of leading for and with compassion?

PART FOUR

BLUEPRINTS FOR AWAKENING COMPASSION AT WORK

Opening space to greet life's tragedies invites disquiet and despair. Awakening compassion calls on our courage. Allowing deep challenges to be gently heard and seen requires sensitivity and presence. Awakening compassion calls on our skill. And greeting the worst of what life offers in the midst of goals, deadlines, and the buzzing demands of busy workplaces makes it all harder. So awakening compassion calls for grace under pressure.[1]

Working with the fragility of emergent patterns in organizations adds to the challenge. Awakening compassion competence calls for honed intuition about groups and systems. To become an architect of compassion is to become savvy about organizational transformation. Compassion architects must believe in and insist on the possibility that workplaces can heal.

To advance the work of compassion architects, we conclude with a set of action tools—or blueprints as we call them—that combine the insights and ideas we have touched on throughout this book. Just as a blueprint guides the process of building a structure, our blueprints guide compassion architects to awaken compassion in their own work and awaken compassion competence in their organizations.

YOUR PERSONAL BLUEPRINT FOR COMPASSION AT WORK

THIS CHAPTER SUPPORTS YOU in creating your personal blueprint for awakening compassion at work. First, a quick assessment highlights your current level of skill with respect to the four parts of the compassion process—noticing, interpreting, feeling, and acting. Then, guided questions show you how to build your compassion capability.

This tool allows you to customize your blueprint by considering what happens in different work teams, units, or divisions that makes it easier or harder to express compassion across these different groups. Over time, changes in your role or status may shift your compassion capability, so remember that you can always come back and create new blueprints as your work changes.

EXPLORE YOUR CURRENT CAPACITY

STEP 1: RATE YOUR SKILLS

➤ Think about the importance of compassion for a specific organization, division, unit, or work group as you read the following statements.

➤ Where are you along each continuum? Rate yourself as far to the right, far to the left, or somewhere in the middle.

	Noticing	
I feel uncomfortable knowing about people's suffering, and would rather keep this awareness out of my work.		I feel comfortable knowing about people's suffering and see this awareness as an important aspect of my work.

	Noticing	
In this group, I seldom have conversations in which I notice another person's suffering.		In this group, I often have conversations in which I notice another person's suffering.

	Interpreting	
In this group, I tend to see people who get behind or make mistakes in their work as problematic and want to get away from them.		In this group, I tend to see people who get behind or make mistakes in their work as in need of help and I approach them.

	Interpreting	
In this group, if I find out that someone is having difficulty in his or her life, I tend to ignore it and keep the focus on tasks.		In this group, if I find out that someone is having difficulty in his or her life, I tend to ask about it and focus on the person's well-being.

	Feeling	
I seldom feel concern for others in this group.		I often feel concern for others in this group.

	Feeling	
I find it difficult to take the perspective of others in this group.		I find it easy to take the perspective of others in this group.

	Acting	
I rarely find myself taking action to help others in this group.		I often find myself taking action to help others in this group.

	Acting	
If I found out that people in this work group were suffering, I would probably not know what to do to comfort them.		If I found out that people in this work group were suffering, I would very likely know what to do to comfort them.

STEP 2: IDENTIFY STRENGTHS AND CHALLENGES

Strengths: Identify the two lines where you rated yourself farthest to the right—these are your strengths. Do they correspond with noticing, interpreting, feeling, or acting?

Challenges: Identify the two lines where you rated yourself farthest to the left—these are your challenges. Do they correspond with noticing, interpreting, feeling, or acting?

CREATE YOUR PERSONAL BLUEPRINT FOR COMPASSION AT WORK

➤ Note below whether each aspect of the compassion process is a strength or a challenge.

➤ If it is a strength, think about how you can build on it to awaken greater compassion in your work.

➤ If it is a challenge, think about how you might strengthen your capacity in this area.

NOTICING SUFFERING

This aspect of compassion tends to be a _____ strength _____ challenge.

Building personal capacity

What could I do to become more comfortable knowing about people's difficulties?

What could I do to make room for suffering to surface?

What could I do to better notice when my colleagues are "not themselves"?

How can I make myself available for deeper conversations where I might be able to notice suffering?

Strengthening group capacity

What makes it difficult in this group to know more about people's lives, including their difficulties?

How could we engage each other differently to make it more likely that people could reveal suffering and we would notice it?

Could we establish or use regular meetings to check in with one another? Could we have more playful times together that might make it easier to notice suffering?

GENEROUSLY INTERPRETING SUFFERING

This aspect of compassion tends to be a _____ strength _____ challenge.

Building personal capacity

What can I do to remind myself that "there's always pain in the room" when I encounter difficult situations at work?

How can I become more comfortable and skilled at asking if something is wrong when I notice that a client or coworker is not "himself" or "herself" on a particular day?

How can I inquire about mistakes, errors, or missed deadlines in ways that do not create blame?

How can I learn more about common forms of suffering that occur in this group and industry, so that I can take them into account?

Strengthening group capacity

How could we create reminders for our group that our members are good, capable, and worthy of compassion?

How could we build more regular interpersonal check-ins into our work so that it is easier to understand and generously interpret what's happening when something is going wrong?

How might we engage each other differently when we experience a failure, so that we regard it as an opportunity to learn?

How can we educate ourselves about the common sources of suffering in the lives of our coworkers and clients so we can understand them more easily?

FEELING EMPATHY AND CONCERN

This aspect of compassion tends to be a _____ strength _____ challenge.

Building personal capacity

How can I remind myself to "stand in the other person's shoes" or see things from his or her perspective, especially during a disagreement or when my expectations are not met?

When I need to tune into other people's feelings, how can I turn off distractions and learn to be more present?

How can I learn new ways to be mindful at work?

How might I learn to be better at listening with empathy and acknowledging my colleagues' stress or suffering, without interrupting or needing to jump in and fix things?

Strengthening group capacity

Can we invent new ways of working together that allow us to be sure that we are hearing one another's perspectives on important issues?

Could we create more retreat-like times or technology-free meetings where we lessen distractions and emphasize listening?

How could we begin and end our group discussions with an emphasis on being mindfully aware and fully present?

Could we consistently acknowledge times when people are encountering stress or going through difficulties?

ACTING TO ALLEVIATE SUFFERING

This aspect of compassion tends to be a _____ strength _____ challenge.

Building personal capacity

How could I better keep track of what would be helpful to each of my colleagues in times of stress or suffering?

How could I cultivate my ability to be present with people who are suffering and acknowledge them in ways that allow my presence to become an act of compassion?

How could I become more comfortable at improvising actions when I learn that someone is suffering?

How could I be more responsive in sharing and responding to calls for action when others alert me that someone is suffering?

Strengthening group capacity

How can we easily and quickly get in touch with each other in case of an emergency or when suffering requires immediate action?

Could we find ways to share more stories of compassion that would inspire us to take action when suffering surfaces?

Could we more regularly recognize the times when members of the group engage in improvisational action to alleviate suffering?

Could we find new ways to share alerts when someone is suffering to draw out more compassionate actions?

YOUR ORGANIZATION'S BLUEPRINT FOR COMPETENCE

HOW DOES AN ENTIRE ORGANIZATION awaken compassion? By developing a social architecture that supports compassion competence. Organizations that *collectively notice, interpret, feel, and act in an effective and customized fashion to alleviate suffering* exhibit compassion competence. This chapter supports you in creating a blueprint for increasing these four dimensions of your organization's compassion competence. First, a quick assessment highlights your current level of skill. You can complete this tool yourself or with others. If you choose to complete it as a group, know that shared perceptions illuminate your strengths, while differing perceptions highlight your opportunities. Use your results to facilitate discussions about enhancing compassion competence throughout your organization or system.

EXPLORE YOUR ORGANIZATION'S CURRENT COMPETENCE

STEP 1: RATE YOUR SKILLS

➤ Think about the importance of compassion for a particular organization, division, unit, or work group as you read the following statements.

➤ Consider your resources, broadly defined as anything that can be used to alleviate suffering. Common resources at work include presence; empathic listening; expressions of concern; helping with running errands, child care, or making meals; flexible time arrangements; task flexibility; donations of material goods; and financial aid.

➤ Where is your organization along each continuum? Rate it as far to the right, far to the left, or somewhere in the middle.

	Speed	
This organization is generally slow to respond to people who are suffering.		This organization is generally quick to respond to people who are suffering.

	Speed	
This organization typically does not direct resources to alleviate suffering if it spans a long time.		This organization typically continues to coordinate resources as conditions change over time.

	Scope	
This organization is not capable of tapping into a breadth of resources to alleviate suffering.		This organization is capable of tapping into a broad array of resources to alleviate suffering.

	Scope	
This group is not good at assessing what would be helpful to alleviate suffering and calibrating resources with needs.		This group is very good at assessing what would be helpful to alleviate suffering and calibrating resources with needs.

	Magnitude	
Over the past year, I do not recall an instance when people were suffering and the organization generated significant resources to help.		Over the past year, I recall several instances when people were suffering and the organization generated significant resources to help.

	Magnitude	
This organization typically directs few resources toward people who are suffering, even if needs are very great.		This organization typically directs many resources toward people who are suffering, matching the resources with what is needed.

	Customization	
We seldom take action to make sure colleagues have what would be uniquely helpful when they experience suffering.		We often take action to make sure colleagues have what would be uniquely helpful when they experience suffering.

	Customization	
It would be uncommon in this organization for people's unique needs and preferences to be addressed when they encounter suffering.		It would be common in this organization for people's unique needs and preferences to be addressed when they encounter suffering.

STEP 2: IDENTIFY STRENGTHS AND CHALLENGES

Strengths: Identify the two lines where you rated your organization farthest to the right—these are your strengths. Do they correspond with speed, scale, magnitude, or customization? What insights does this generate?

Challenges: Identify the two lines where you rated your organization farthest to the left—these are your challenges. Do they correspond with speed, scale, magnitude, or customization? What insights does this generate?

CREATE YOUR ORGANIZATION'S BLUEPRINT FOR COMPETENCE

➤ Note below whether each measure is a strength or challenge.

➤ Explore the strategy and action questions to determine how you will build on your strengths and mitigate your challenges to increase your organization's compassion competence.

SPEED

This dimension of competence is a _____ strength _____ challenge.

Strategy questions

When a compassionate response to suffering begins immediately after we learn of it, what aspects of the organization make it respond quickly?

How could we increase the speed with which we gather information about suffering?

What slows down our responses to suffering?

Action questions

What actions can we take to further increase the speed with which our system responds to suffering?

What can we do as a group to quickly adjust to needs as they change over time?

Who will take action? By when?

Who else do we need to involve in this initiative to increase the speed with which our system responds to suffering?

SCOPE

This dimension of competence is a _____ strength _____ challenge.

Strategy questions

What resources do we tap most often? What resources are we missing?

Could we expand the breadth of resources we regard as relevant and possible to generate in the organization?

How could we more easily assess what range of resources would be helpful when someone is suffering?

Could we share information about suffering in ways that would bring out a broader array of resources?

Action questions

What actions can we take now to increase the breadth of resources our system generates in response to suffering?

What can we do as a group to calibrate resources to needs as they change over time?

Who will take action? By when?

Who else do we need to involve in this initiative to increase the scope of our response to suffering?

MAGNITUDE

This dimension of competence is a _____ strength _____ challenge.

Strategy questions

What can we learn from our experiences with generating too few resources?

What can we learn about our organization's experiences in generating too many resources?

How can we better coordinate our efforts to "turn on" and "turn off" the resources as conditions change over time?

Action questions

What actions can we take now to increase the magnitude of resources our system generates in response to suffering?

What can we do as a group to match the magnitude of resources to needs as they change over time?

Who will take action? By when?

Who else do we need to involve in this initiative to increase the magnitude of our response to suffering?

CUSTOMIZATION

This dimension of competence is a _____ strength _____ challenge.

Strategy questions

Looking at past experiences of suffering and compassion, what do we see about how we were able to individualize resources to the needs and preferences of those who were suffering?

How can we involve the people who hold reliable knowledge about needs and preferences so we can more easily customize?

How can we better coordinate to customize resources quickly?

Action questions

What specific actions can we take now to increase our ability to customize resources in response to suffering?

What can we do as a group to continue to customize resources to needs as they change over time?

Who will take action? By when?

Who else do we need to involve in this initiative to increase the capacity of our system to customize resources in response to suffering?

A BLUEPRINT FOR YOUR SOCIAL ARCHITECTURE

This tool incorporates the design principles for compassion architects from chapter 9 to guide you in redesigning specific elements of your organization, such as networks, culture, roles, routines, and leadership actions that shape the way it responds to suffering. Use this blueprint to make it more likely that every time suffering surfaces, your organization will respond with compassion.

EXPLORE YOUR ORGANIZATION'S SOCIAL ARCHITECTURE

STEP 1: RATE YOUR ORGANIZATION'S SOCIAL ARCHITECTURE

> Where is your organization's social architecture along each continuum? Rate it as far to the right, far to the left, or somewhere in the middle.

	Networks	
This organization is characterized by a few small clusters of people who know each other well.		This organization is characterized by many small clusters of people who know each other well.

	Networks	
The quality of relationships in this organization is low.		The quality of relationships in this organization is high.

	Culture	
The values of this organization emphasize profit or efficiency more than anything else.		The values of this organization emphasize the importance of people as well as profit or efficiency.

	Culture	
This organization does not value the humanity of its people or its clients much.		This organization values the humanity of its people and its clients to a great degree.

	Roles	
People here feel little responsibility for taking care of others as part of their work.		People here feel a great deal of responsibility for taking care of others as part of their work.

	Roles	
I do not perceive a very great deal of autonomy and creativity in the way people craft their roles in this organization.		I perceive a great deal of autonomy and creativity in the way that people craft their roles in this organization.

	Routines	
Decisions get made here in ways that do not reflect much care for people.		Decisions get made here in ways that reflect a great care for people.

	Routines	
The way that we hire, onboard, train, develop, and reward for performance incorporates little focus on care for people.		The way that we hire, onboard, train, develop, and reward for performance incorporates significant focus on care for people.

I do not recall many instances when a leader called for compassion in this organization.	*Leadership*	I recall several instances when a leader called for compassion in this organization.
The leaders in this organization do not model care or concern as a primary part of work.	*Leadership*	The leaders in this organization model care and concern as a primary part of work.
I rarely hear stories of compassion in this organization.	*Stories*	I often hear stories of compassion in this organization.
I can't remember ever hearing a legendary story of compassion that everyone in this organization would recognize.	*Stories*	I can easily remember and tell a legendary story of compassion that everyone in this organization would recognize.

STEP 2: IDENTIFY FACILITATORS AND BLOCKS

Facilitators: Identify the two lines where you rated your social architecture farthest to the right—these are your facilitators. Do they correspond to networks, culture, roles, routines, leadership, or stories?

Blocks: Identify the two lines where you rated your organization farthest to the left—these are your blocks. Do they correspond to networks, culture, roles, routines, leadership, or stories?

CREATE A BLUEPRINT FOR YOUR SOCIAL ARCHITECTURE

➤ Note below whether each element of your social architecture is facilitating or blocking compassion in your organization.

➤ Focus your attention first on your facilitators, discussing how you can make them more consistent or reliable.

➤ Then turn your attention to your blocks, discussing how you can mitigate them.

NETWORKS

The networks in our organization are _____ facilitating _____ blocking compassion.

Design principles related to networks

➤ Create subnetworks within the organization where people can identify with one another and be more fully and authentically known.

➤ Invite stakeholders to dialogue about important issues to open up different points of view.

➤ Build on your connections. When suffering surfaces, offer your presence, your willingness to listen, and a simple acknowledgment that you are with the other person amid the pain.

➤ Draw more people into compassionate action and encourage them to generate and calibrate resources.

➤ When suffering requires elaborate patterns of improvised action, match those who are suffering with a buddy who can monitor their well-being and adjust the pattern in a quick, mindful way.

Changes to our organization's social architecture

How might we form small networks of people across the organization who know each other well and share common interests?

How might we increase the quality of connections in these networks?

How might we invite more stakeholders to participate in regular dialogues to build empathy?

What other changes can we make to leverage strengths in our organization's networks?

How might we mitigate blocks to compassion in our organization's networks?

CULTURE

The culture in our organization is _____ facilitating _____ blocking compassion.

Design principles related to culture

> ➤ Regard any organizational change that improves efficiency as an opportunity to simultaneously increase compassion by tying the change to the value of shared humanity.

> ➤ Point out the cost of corrosive connections and actions that undermine the cultural value of shared humanity.

> ➤ Articulate the cultural assumption of shared humanity in a way that makes sense in your work. Use this statement to guide how you and others engage when conflicts or disagreements erupt.

> ➤ Set aspirational community goals that help people see that their success is tied to their interdependence in a human ecosystem where everyone is striving for compassion.

> ➤ Involve people in sharing their personal experiences of compassion at work as a way to heighten empathy.

> ➤ Host retreats or gatherings that engage people in playful interactions with symbols of compassion and explore how they relate to their work as a means of increasing empathy.

Changes to the social architecture

How might we further develop assumptions of shared humanity in our culture?

How might we articulate values and put them into action in ways that reflect shared humanity and support compassion?

How might we make it more normal to express emotion, respect, affection, and care in the organization?

How might we incorporate more play into our work in appropriate ways?

How might we leverage other strengths of our culture to support compassion?

How might we mitigate blocks to compassion that originate in our culture?

ROLES

The roles in our organization are _____ facilitating _____ blocking compassion.

Design principles related to roles

> Regard any organizational change that improves efficiency as an opportunity to simultaneously increase compassion by redesigning roles in ways that elevate people's sense of responsibility for others' well-being.

> Invent roles that address persistent sources of suffering at work.

> Describe all roles so they include explicit responsibility not only for protecting the organization but also for protecting the well-being of stakeholders.

> Support and reward the emergent roles that happen during compassionate action, such as coordinators or expeditors who make action more predictable and enhance the competence in the system.

Changes to the social architecture

How might we redesign work roles to expand responsibility for others' well-being?

How might we encourage people to take initiative in expanding their roles to include responsibility for others' well-being?

How might we invent roles that would address the most common forms of suffering in the system?

How might we better spot and recognize emergent roles that increase competence in the system?

What changes could we make to leverage the strengths of roles in our organization?

What changes would mitigate blocks to compassion that originate in our role definitions?

ROUTINES

The routines in our organization are _____ facilitating _____ blocking compassion.

Design principles related to routines

➤ Revamp selection and hiring routines to emphasize high-quality connections, empathy, and fit with the cultural assumptions and values of shared humanity at work.

➤ Create meeting or gathering routines that bring people into regular, consistent contact with each other and make space to discuss both work performance and relational needs for help or support.

➤ Emphasize informal recognition and formal social recognition of compassionate actions in ways that make compassion rewarding rather than costly.

➤ Invent training routines that address persistent sources of suffering in work.

➤ Celebrate compassionate action regularly with celebration routines that strengthen relationships and reinforce people's belief in the compassion of the organization.

➤ Institute routines for discussing errors, failures, mistakes, and near misses in ways that emphasize learning and reduce blame.

➤ When decisions involve responding to suffering, discuss the decision from the point of view of multiple roles within and outside the organization and actively consider the perspectives of others who are involved.

➤ Develop frameworks and routines for decision-making, including measures and data tracking that make visible the costs of suffering and the value of human dignity.

➤ Adopt formal routines for inviting all stakeholders to participate in dialogue regarding important issues to reveal multiple perspectives.

➤ Involve clients and customers in appropriately playful engagement with the organization or its product-development routines.

➤ When suffering requires sustained responsiveness, use a short daily meeting or check-in as a way to ensure that improvised actions are coordinated and that they continue to remain coordinated over time as conditions change.

Changes to the social architecture that will leverage strengths or mitigate blocks

How might we shift the way that we do recruiting, hiring, onboarding, off-boarding, performance management, conflict resolution, and other human resource routines to infuse them with more compassion?

How might we shift routines about our regular meetings to emphasize shared humanity and compassion?

How might we shift training and professional development to incorporate more skills related to compassion?

How might we shift the way we informally and formally recognize and reward people so that we are increasing the rewards for compassion?

How might we shift the way we plan and make decisions to incorporate greater emphasis on human worth and dignity?

How might we shift the way we routinely use communication channels to enhance empathy and compassion?

How might we leverage other strengths in our organization's routines?

How might we mitigate blocks to compassion that are a result of our organization's routines?

LEADERS' ACTIONS AND STORIES

Leaders' actions and stories in our organization are _____ facilitating _____ blocking compassion.

Design principles related to stories and leaders' actions

➤ Coach leaders to model compassion and related values in action.

➤ Uphold models of leading with compassion. Share stories of compassionate decisions. Use them to spark discussions about how everyone's roles can be recrafted to incorporate more responsibility for the well-being of others.

➤ Share stories of times when a lack of generous interpretations of errors have caused suffering in the organization, to show how generous interpretations can alleviate this suffering.

➤ Draw people into imagining new ways that they could collectively respond to problems or difficulties by telling stories about how the response could be more fun and engaging.

➤ Tell stories of improvised compassionate action as a way to inspire greater participation and expand emergent patterns.

➤ Tap into pride and elevation that motivate people to engage in compassion by sharing stories that expand people's view of what is possible.

Changes to the social architecture that will leverage strengths or mitigate blocks

How might we elevate and showcase more leaders as role models for compassion at work?

How might we enable leaders to draw people into rituals when suffering strikes?

How might we learn to lead discussions of errors and mistakes that emphasize learning and compassion?

How might we share stories of compassion in the organization more authentically?

How can we leverage the strengths of stories in our organization?

How might we mitigate the blocks that originate from leaders' actions or stories in our organization?

13

OVERCOMING
OBSTACLES TO
COMPASSION AT WORK

JUST AS THE POSSIBILITY OF human responsiveness to pain is inherent in every system, so too is the possibility that we will turn away from suffering. Throughout this book we have offered numerous examples of failures of compassion at work and the gullies they carve in people's sense of how much of themselves they can bring to work, how much they can trust those around them, and how committed and engaged they will be in their workplace. In this chapter, we summarize the most common obstacles to compassion in organizations and offer tools for overcoming them.

HEARTS TURNED TO STONE

Here are the six most common obstacles to compassion that arise in an organization's social architecture:

1. When ties between people are characterized by incivility, disrespect, or a sense of injustice, it is far less likely that networks can be activated in the service of compassion.

2. When self-interest is at the core of an organization's culture with little emphasis on values that support shared humanity or the common good, it is far less likely that people will regard others' suffering as relevant or worthy of their attention and effort.

3. When systems feature roles that emphasize self-oriented responsibilities or focus solely on protecting the organization from risk, it is far less likely that people will view others' well-being as part of their work. When systems offer little room for creative job crafting, it is far less likely that people who are motivated to build compassion into their work will find acceptable ways to do so.

4. When organizations and leaders easily generate blame for anything that goes wrong, it is far less likely that people will engage in generous interpretations of failures, errors, missed deadlines, absences, or other circumstances where suffering arises.

5. When overload and overwork mark the routines that characterize a workplace, it is more likely that people will experience "empathy fatigue," a form of emotional exhaustion in which our capacity to connect with others is diminished.[1] Empathy fatigue makes it far less likely that they will notice suffering, limits feelings of concern, and dampens people's creativity and flexibility in improvising actions to alleviate suffering.

6. When an organization is led by someone who models self-interest and when a system is dominated by stories of a lack of compassion, the leader's actions and stories amplify

the other obstacles. Leaders who model a lack of compassion become barriers to mobilizing resources in response to suffering. Stories that spread the value of an extremely self-interested view or a punitive approach to suffering drive compassion out of an organizational environment, even one with a mission of compassion.[2]

These six obstacles can turn our hearts to stone. In the following section, we shed more light on them and invite you to create a blueprint for overcoming them. Our colleague Arne Carlsen reminds us how we can use "the sensuous experience of being in a mystery" to renew our wonder at compassion when the world threatens to harden our hearts. "Wonder underpins all imagination, empathy, and deep interest in anything beyond self."[3]

Have I ever experienced compassion as a window of light in the darkness? Can I challenge myself to notice more of the compassion I have been overlooking as part of everyday working life? How does beholding others and my workplace in this way inspire me?

WHEN TIES BETWEEN PEOPLE CREATE OBSTACLES

We have seen how important it can be that the ties between people in an organization's networks are plentiful and characterized by respect and trust, so that people identify with each other and have a sense of being seen, valued, and known. But often networks have the opposite effect, isolating and disconnecting people or trapping them in corrosive connections characterized by incivility, disrespect, or injustice.[4]

We met Dr. Arnav through our research on compassion in health care. He recounted a situation that had occurred many years earlier. As a young physician, Dr. Arnav was assigned to the overnight shift in the ER in his hospital, often working alone. The rigid status hierarchy made it almost impossible for him to connect with others on the staff, and he found the night shift lonely. Because of the hospital's location, being on the night shift often meant working with patients who were homeless, suffering from addiction or drug overdoses, or victims of trauma on the city streets. Answering a page one night, Dr. Arnav entered a curtained area of the busy ER to find a large man who made the hospital gurney look small. A wound on his arm had filled with fluid that needed to be drained. Injection tracks patterned the man's forearm, testifying to his addiction. As Dr. Arnav inspected the wound and turned to get equipment to treat it, he remembered muttering under his breath: "Damn druggies."

The mutter wasn't quiet enough. As he left the room, Dr. Arnav felt uneasy and tried to push his feeling away. He rationalized that the addict might have been too out of it to notice. But when he returned with the necessary equipment, Dr. Arnav was surprised to find the man standing beside the bed. He held out his hand. "I'm Anthony," he said. Dr. Arnav froze, as if he'd never shaken a hand before. "What's your name?" Anthony asked.

As Dr. Arnav slowly reached out to shake Anthony's hand, Anthony continued to speak: "I was born in this hospital, probably long before you were born, Dr. Arnav. My mother was a nurse. I never knew my father." He continued, "I've probably been doing drugs since before you were born, too. And yes, I guess from your point of view, I'm just a damn druggie. But that doesn't mean I'm not a human being."

For just a moment, the social architecture of Dr. Arnav's work shifted. No longer was he in a system where patients were numbers. No longer did his power and status in the hierarchy confer the ability to treat others with disrespect with few consequences. Anthony's insistence on being granted humanity and dignity forced a change.

After this encounter, Dr. Arnav told us, he devoted himself to changing his approach to patients and to changing his organization. He learned an important lesson about awakening compassion in his work. Though he thought of himself as a healer, Dr. Arnav realized that his isolation in the hierarchical networks of the hospital, combined with his position of power, had allowed him to disregard the humanity of other staff members, not to mention poor, homeless, or drug-addicted patients who were in need of care. Dr. Arnav began to work with organizations that advocated for the homeless, and he went out of his way to learn more about the conditions of others' lives, confronting his internalized stereotypes about the laziness of people in poverty. He actively worked to take a stance that allowed for more generous interpretations of suffering, and he renewed in himself a personal value of embracing all people in a circle of concern. Dr. Arnav worked as a compassion architect for his hospital, advocating for new forms of care for patients in poverty and for support teams for physicians and nurses on the front lines. For Dr. Arnav and those who joined him, mindfully confronting the obstacles to compassion presented by a cultural tolerance for incivility and disrespect kept their hearts from turning to stone.

Can you identify a time when you missed an opportunity to give or receive compassion at work because the ties between people were characterized by incivility, disrespect, or injustice?

WHEN AN ORGANIZATION'S CULTURE CREATES OBSTACLES

Philosopher and social theorist Martha Nussbaum reminds us that "social institutions . . . construct the shape compassion will take."[5] We have seen how important an organization's cultural assumptions and values of shared humanity are for awakening compassion competence. Let's look now at what can happen when an organization's culture instead turns hearts to stone.

In an investigative exposé of the Enron Corporation, journalists Bethany McLean and Peter Elkind described such a culture.[6] They detail how CEO Kenneth Lay responded to traders who were illegally investing in the oil market and diverting money into offshore accounts by encouraging them to keep generating money, later denying any knowledge of their wrongdoing to protect his position. Lay also hired Jeffrey Skilling to transform Enron into an energy trading firm. Skilling instituted a process nicknamed "rank and yank," whereby employees ruthlessly graded one another, and the bottom 15 percent were fired annually. Skilling's lieutenants, who became known as "the guys with spikes," were charged with reinforcing a highly competitive and brutal working environment. Lay, Skilling, and other executives across the company began taking advantage of opportunities to artificially and illegally inflate the stock price. As they did this, they cashed in their options and quickly built their personal wealth, while simultaneously encouraging lower-level employees to invest their savings and retirement funds in Enron stock. All the while, the organization and its leaders knowingly invested in shell companies to hide burgeoning debt, bankrupting the company. The tragic result was that many employees lost their life savings along with their jobs when Enron collapsed.

We might see this example as an extreme opposite case of the story of Zeke—where an organization engaged in numerous ways to awaken compassion competence on behalf of a lower-level employee. In the Enron example, organizational values that emphasized competition and ruthlessness—coupled with the leaders who modeled and preached extreme self-interest—resulted in an organization that heaped suffering on its members.

∞

Have you ever witnessed a missed opportunity for compassion because strong self-interest took over in your organization? Have you ever missed an opportunity to give or receive compassion because of competition at work?

WHEN ROLES BECOME OBSTACLES

Just as roles can be a powerful source for awakening compassion, they can be formidable obstacles as well. Organizational researchers Andy Molinsky, Adam Grant, and Joshua Margolis created a study in which executives responded in writing to work scenarios where suffering might play a part.[7] They first unscrambled sentences of jumbled words, which served to prime them for what came next. Some of these sentences were neutral (the control condition), while others were designed to activate a professional role script infused with the economic logic of business. In the neutral condition, executives received sentences such as "blue the is sky," which they unscrambled to "the sky is blue." In the economic logic condition, executives received sentences such as "high they profits earn," which they unscrambled to "they earn high profits."

After this priming task, the executives responded to a story by writing a note to Sasha, a hypothetical, highly competent employee who sometimes was late for morning meetings because she didn't have a car. The executives who had unscrambled neutral sentences wrote significantly more compassionate notes to Sasha than the executives who had been primed with scripts that emphasized economic logic. The executives who wrote less compassionate notes also scored lower on a measure of empathy. How we construe our roles and the meaning we hold about our responsibilities matters mightily for how much empathy and compassion will become part of our normal work.

Have you ever missed an opportunity for compassion at work because you felt that it wasn't professional to express emotion or care for someone? Have you seen others miss opportunities for compassion because compassion wasn't seen as part of the job?

WHEN ROUTINES CREATE OBSTACLES

We have explored the power of putting organizational routines in the service of compassion. Work routines, however, can also contribute to tremendous fatigue. Work can create *compassion fatigue*, a condition in which we experience secondary trauma by witnessing the trauma of others.[8] When our work brings us into contact with suffering, if we don't rest and recover, we can turn our hearts to stone.

In her book *Alone Together*, anthropologist Sherry Turkle relays a story of a museum curator, Diane, who gave up her evenings and weekends to work, consistently using her handheld device until two in the morning. Diane described the effect of a cacophony of demands: "I don't sleep well, but I still can't keep up with what is sent to me. Now for work, I'm expected to have a Twitter feed and a

Facebook presence about the museum. And do a blog on museum happenings. . . . I keep losing my voice. It's not from talking too much. All I do is type, but it has hit me at my voice. The doctor says it's a nervous thing."[9]

In response to this cacophony, Diane tried to erase her humanity and turn herself into a "maximizing machine." Her empathy for others (and herself) was quickly exhausted by hundreds of emails and text messages along with the meetings and phone calls that cluttered her days. Also driven out were generous interpretations that might come from inquiring about what was happening to others or her sensitivity to small details that might reveal suffering.

In our research, Ning told us a similar and deeply personal story:

> I gave birth to a stillborn baby girl. I work in child care, and I was very nervous about going back to work. The other teachers in my school asked me to help with the infant care unit after just being back at work a few days, because someone had called in sick and they needed help. I knew that I couldn't do it. I wasn't ready. Sadly the people I was working with were not compassionate. They were busy and they felt I should take my turn to substitute in the infant care unit. I approached the head manager and told her that I was willing to resign my position immediately.

Luckily, Ning's manager was not drowning in compassion fatigue or lost in the same cacophony of work demands. She quickly grasped the depth of Ning's loss and exempted her from substituting on the infant care unit.[10] Being deafened by a cacophony of demands, buried under an endless pile of emails, or tangled in a web of deadlines often blinds us to the suffering of others.

∞

Have you missed an opportunity for compassion at work because you felt overloaded, distracted, overwhelmed, or under such pressure that you did not notice others? Have you witnessed missed opportunities for compassion in your workplace because people were too burdened or burned out to feel empathy and act with compassion?

WHEN LEADERSHIP CREATES OBSTACLES

When leaders fail to acknowledge suffering, the silence often leaves the members of an organization uncertain about how to interpret and handle difficult situations. In chapter 10, we saw the example of Bruce Shepard bravely breaking the silence that so often surrounds suicide in work communities, but we have seen many organizations where talk of suicide was swept under the rug, leaving people mute, their suffering unacknowledged.

When leaders treat others in the organization as if they are not worthy of respect, especially in the face of errors and failures, compassion drains from a system quickly. We saw this in one corporate setting we observed. Monica remembered witnessing this corrosive leadership. She recounted:

> I was sitting in a large shared workspace called a bullpen watching a marketing team go about their daily work. They were focused on a spreadsheet, trying to manage a budget problem. An executive, who I will call Doug, had not attended the daily work huddle and did not seem to know or care about the team's urgent need to focus on the budget. He walked briskly into the bullpen demanding a status update about a website project. He began to fire questions at

people in a loud, brash voice. People answered as best they could, but the interaction was a jarring interruption to their focus. Doug wasn't happy with the answers he was getting, so his voice grew louder and angrier. The quiet efficiency that had characterized the bullpen was shattered. People scrambled but attempted to avoid catching Doug's eye. He walked toward one person's workstation, took a look at a prototype web design on her computer, and started to swear about the design imperfections. "Where the f--k is Vince?" he yelled, looking for the graphic designer. "This is all his fault." People looked on in silence, no one knowing what to say. Just then Doug's administrative assistant Julie walked into the space to give the team some updated budget information. Doug abruptly shouted at her, "Shut up. Can't you see I'm busy?" Turning his back on the team and Julie, he stormed out of the bullpen. Everyone could hear Doug's voice as he walked away, saying, "What a worthless pile of s--t. Heads are going to roll."

It is all too easy for leaders who lose sight of how they are treating lower-level people in organizations to leave a trail of suffering in their wake. Philosopher Martha Nussbaum reminds us of the central responsibility of leaders not to lose sight of the humanity they share with others: "The misfortunes to which compassion commonly responds—deaths, wounds, losses of loved ones, losses of citizenship, hunger, poverty—are real and general. They really are the common lot of all human beings. Thus the kings who deny that the lot of the peasant could be theirs are deceiving themselves."[11]

∞

Have you witnessed a missed opportunity for compassion in your organization because a leader was not paying attention or not

willing to acknowledge suffering? Have you missed opportunities
for compassion because you were blinded by power to the
condition of others?

REWRITING MISSED OPPORTUNITIES TO OVERCOME OBSTACLES

Missed opportunities for compassion often become opportunities for regret. Compassion writers Daniel Homan and Lonni Collins Pratt remind us that while it may be "heartbreaking to hear the pain of strangers, it also opens up the heart of human-focused work and infuses it with meaning."[12] It can be painful to look at missed opportunities for compassion and see how work threatens to turn our hearts to stone. But finding the courage to turn toward these stories and rewrite them offers us the possibility of change.[13] This final blueprint harnesses the power of rewriting missed opportunities for compassion, using them to catalyze change. As Daniel Homan and Lonni Collins Pratt say, "You can't engage with human pain and remain unchanged. But that is the beauty of it. . . . In taking on the pain of others we act in the transformation of the world."[14]

CREATE A BLUEPRINT FOR OVERCOMING OBSTACLES TO COMPASSION

STEP 1: IDENTIFY YOUR MOST COMPELLING STORY

➤ Step back and look over all of the missed opportunities for compassion that you have recalled as you read this chapter.

➤ Identify the one that represents an obstacle you would most like to overcome.

STEP 2: REWRITE THE STORY

➤ Tell the story as it would happen if compassion had been present. How would the story unfold differently?

➤ Identify the main elements that would need to change to make your new story true. How did incivility, toxic culture, narrow role definitions, exhausting routines, or insensitive leadership contribute?

➤ Make a list of what would need to change for this new story of compassion to be plausible in your organization.

STEP 3: SPRINGBOARD TO CATALYZE ACTION

➤ Use the missed opportunity as a springboard to action. Learn to tell the story of the missed opportunity compellingly, to draw people into the need for compassion and convey the suffering that happens without it.

➤ Add a call to action that builds on your rewritten story and conveys your vision.

➤ Add skills to your personal development plan that will enable you to do what is needed to help overcome these obstacles to compassion in your work.

➤ Identify the other people you must influence in order to create and sustain conditions that would transform this obstacle in your organization.

➤ Make a plan to approach influencers. How will you use your story to help them see the necessity, power, and beauty of greater compassion competence in your system?

EPILOGUE:
A CALL TO
AWAKEN

COMPASSION TEACHER PEMA CHÖDRÖN calls people to the urgent need for compassion in the world now when she asserts that "awakening is no longer a luxury or an ideal."[1] She is echoing the call from His Holiness the Dalai Lama, as quoted in the foreword of this book by Raj Sisodia, who reminds us that the cultivation of compassion is a necessity if our species is to survive.

We too have demonstrated that compassion at work is neither a luxury nor an ideal. Organizations cannot afford the hidden costs to human capability that come from perpetuating suffering. In desperate need of new sources of adaptability, collaboration, innovation, quality, and engagement, workplaces must turn toward making compassion at work a reality. But awakening compassion competence requires breaking out of a prison of self-interest, a point underscored by compassion scientist Emma Seppälä as she shows us that it is compassion that leads toward true happiness.[2] Albert Einstein called our fascination with self-interest an optical delusion:

A human being is a part of the whole called by us "Universe," a part limited in time and space. He experiences himself, his thoughts and feelings as something separate from the rest—a kind of optical delusion of his consciousness. This delusion is a kind of prison for us, restricting us to our personal desires and to affection for a few persons nearest us. Our task must be to free ourselves from this prison by widening our circles of compassion to embrace all living creatures and the whole of nature in its beauty.[3]

In stories and examples from a variety of industries, and in work roles that span from billing clerk to president and chief executive officer, we've illustrated the quiet power of compassion at work to widen our circles of concern. We have seen how organizations as human communities are the house of suffering. And we have witnessed that though they are filled with the tragedies, losses, and indignities that beset us, they are also filled with responses to those tragedies that may save us. We have found that studying compassion is an adventure in wonder. We hope that through this book you discover and embark on that adventure as well.

THE QUIET POWER TO ELEVATE PEOPLE AND ORGANIZATIONS

Sociologist Robert Wuthnow wrote of the power of compassion to elevate people and organizations: "Compassion enriches us and ennobles us, even those of us who are neither the caregivers nor the recipients, because it holds forth a vision of what good society can be."[4] While words like *wonder, beauty,* and *compassion* aren't usually lauded as part of work or leadership, they should be. Scholars Nancy Adler and André Delbecq, like the leaders we met in chapter 10, point out the power of renewing our belief in the beauty of compassion to find our way in a fractured world where "leadership is not a place where suffering is avoided or courage is unnecessary."[5] Being held by the compassion of colleagues renews our hope and belief in the best of what human work and organizations can be.

Compassion at work calls us to remember that suffering is rarely a problem to be solved. Rashid, a consultant we met in our research, became hopeless after the loss of his child: "My daughter died in a stupid, needless car accident, and I thought my life was over. I wanted to keep myself from committing suicide, so I threw myself into my work." Nothing could resolve the pain of Rashid's loss. At times like this, our colleague Lloyd Sandelands offers a useful distinction between *seeing* and *beholding*.[6] This distinction reminds us of the danger of seeing people as problems to solve. When we do, we turn people like Rashid into objects to be managed and manipulated. Seeing suffering as something to fix, we rarely rise to the level of compassion. Only when we call upon the human capacity to behold do we find our way to the quiet power of compassion.

To behold Rashid and others like him whose suffering drains hope and purpose from their lives is to literally hold them in the light of our minds and hearts in ways that celebrate and illuminate their intrinsic worth and beauty. Leaders like Bruce Shepard and Pat Christen showed us how to behold the beauty of fragile, complex human beings in the midst of great suffering. To behold another helps us open the door to that mystery of our presence as a salve that can comfort.[7] At moments when we desperately don't know what to do for someone like Rashid, or for our own hopelessness and despair, we can turn to the quiet power of compassion. Rashid found unexpected healing in the way his colleagues were able to behold his suffering with compassion: "The people here were incredible. They gave me space when I needed it, but they didn't let me be alone. This organization saved my life."

This lifesaving, life-giving power might be why the poet John O'Donohue compared compassion to a window of light in the darkness. It might be why geophysicist Xavier Le Pichon, who discovered the fragility of the Earth's tectonic plates, sees the same radical discovery at "the heart of humanity."[8] It might be why Stanford neurosurgeon James Doty, founder of the groundbreaking Center for Compassion and Altruism Research and Education there, says, "We are at the beginning of an age of compassion. Right now it's a ripple in human consciousness fueled by compassion, but it's a ripple that has the potential to become a tsunami."[9]

When we regard the quiet power of compassion as a call to a whole new way of being, we change our work in ways that are both tiny and vast. We pick up on small clues when something is amiss. We ask a delicate question with sensitivity. We are willing to close the door, turn off the phone, and create safe space for emotions to emerge. We reject cultures of brutality. We embrace goals of stewardship. We no longer shrink from compassion as part of our work role, whether we clean the floors or fly the planes or lead the troops. The lifesaving, life-giving power of compassion to elevate people and organizations makes it everyone's job.

Whether it is small and private or immense and public, beholding suffering with compassion sparks a sense of wonder and beauty, renewing our belief in what is possible in organizations. And in the face of obstacles so huge that they threaten to close us down completely, insisting on the transformational potential of compassion in workplaces becomes an act of radical possibility. So the challenge is no longer to find a good reason that compassion matters for business. The challenge now is to heed the call to design work and workplaces that awaken compassion.

NOTES

PART ONE: An Introduction to Suffering, Compassion, and Work

1. Peter Frost, "Why Compassion Counts!" *Journal of Management Inquiry* 20, no. 4 (December 2011): 395–401.

CHAPTER 1: What Is Compassion at Work?

1. You will find downloadable research reports and summaries of our work at CompassionLab.org.

2. Jane E. Dutton, Kristina M. Workman, and Ashley E. Hardin, "Compassion at Work," *Annual Review of Organizational Psychology and Organizational Behavior* 1 (March 2014): 277–304.

3. Two summaries: Martin E. P. Seligman, *Flourish: A Visionary New Understanding of Happiness and Well-Being* (New York: Free Press, 2011); Barbara Fredrickson, *Positivity* (New York: Crown Publishers, 2009).

4. Stephanie L. Brown, R. Michael Brown, and Louis A. Penner, *Moving Beyond Self-Interest: Perspectives from Evolutionary Biology, Neuroscience, and the Social Sciences* (New York: Oxford University Press, 2011).

5. We researched common forms of suffering in Jacoba M. Lilius, Monica C. Worline, Sally Maitlis, Jason Kanov, Jane E. Dutton, and Peter Frost, "The contours and consequences of compassion at work," *Journal of Organizational Behavior* 29, no. 2 (February 2008): 193–218.

6. This was a main focus of a book by our longtime colleague Peter Frost, *Toxic Emotions at Work and What You Can Do About Them* (Boston: Harvard Business School Press, 2003).

CHAPTER 2: Does Compassion at Work Really Matter?

1. Kim S. Cameron, David Bright, and Arran Caza, "Exploring the Relationship between Organizational Virtuousness and Performance," *American Behavioral Scientist* 47, no. 6 (February 2004): 766–90.

2. Kim Cameron, Carlos Mora, Trevor Leutscher, and Margaret Calarco, "Effects of Positive Practices on Organizational Effectiveness," *Journal of Applied Behavioral Science* 47, no. 3 (January 26, 2011): 266–308. doi: 10.1177/0021886310395514.

3. Quoted in "Who Cared?" Gallup, Business Journal, page 1, http://www.gallup.com/businessjournal/427/Who-Cared.aspx?g_source=Who%20cared&g_medium=search&g_campaign=tiles.

4. For a summary, see Jay Barney, "Looking Inside for Competitive Advantage," *Academy of Management Executive* 9, no. 4 (1995): 49–61.

5. For more information, see Jennifer Robison, "How the Ritz-Carlton Manages the Mystique," Gallup, Business Journal, http://www.gallup.com/business-journal/112906/how-ritzcarlton-manages-mystique.aspx.

6. Pablo Zoghbi-Manrique-de-Lara and Rita Guerra-Baez, "Exploring the Influence of Ethical Climate on Employee Compassion in the Hospitality Industry," *Journal of Business Ethics* 133, no. 3 (February 2016): 605–17.

7. Stephanie O'Donohoe and Darach Turley, "Compassion at the counter: Service providers and bereaved consumers," *Human Relations* 59, no. 1 (October 2006): 1429–48.

8. Quoted in Nina Simosko, "Leading Innovation in the Workplace. First Step: Cultivate Compassion," NTT Innovation Institute, Inc. (blog), October 6, 2015, http://www.ntti3.com/blog/leading-innovation-in-the-workplace-first-step-cultivate-compassion/.

9. Toyah L. Miller, Matthew G. Grimes, Jeffery S. McMullen, and Timothy J. Vogus, "Venturing for Others with Heart and Head: How Compassion Encourages Social Entrepreneurship," *Academy of Management Review* 37, no. 4 (October 1, 2012): 616–40.

10. For an overview, see Dorothy Leonard and Jeffrey F. Rayport, "Spark Innovation Through Empathic Design," *Harvard Business Review* (November–December 1997), https://hbr.org/1997/11/spark-innovation-through-empathic-design. See also Dev Patnaik, *Wired to Care: How Companies Prosper When They Create Widespread Empathy* (Upper Saddle River, NJ: FT Press, 2009).

11. Pavithra Mehta and Suchitra Shenoy, *Infinite Vision: How Aravind Became the World's Greatest Business Case for Compassion* (San Francisco: Berrett-Koehler Publishers, 2011), 5.

12. Amy Edmondson, "Learning from Mistakes Is Easier Said Than Done: Group and Organizational Influences on the Detection and Correction of Human Error," *Journal of Applied Behavioral Science* 32, no. 1 (1996): 5–28.

13. Read about this unexpected finding in Amy Edmondson, *Teaming: How Organizations Learn, Innovate, and Compete in the Knowledge Economy* (San Francisco: Jossey-Bass, 2012).

14. For an overview, see Alec Appelbaum, "The Constant Consumer," Gallup, Business Journal, modified June 17, 2001, http://www.gallup.com/business-journal/745/constant-customer.aspx.

15. This framework comes from Sharon C. Bolton, "Who cares? Offering emotion work as a 'gift' in the nursing labour process," *Journal of Advanced Nursing* 32, no. 3 (September 2000): 580–86.

16. Jacoba M. Lilius, "Recovery at Work: Understanding the Restorative Side of 'Depleting' Client Interactions," *Academy of Management Review* 37, no. 4 (2012): 569–88.

17. Arlie R. Hochschild, *The Managed Heart: Commercialization of Human Feeling* (Berkeley: University of California Press, 1983).

18. This definition comes from Ken G. Smith, Stephen J. Carroll, and Susan J. Ashford, "Intra- and Interorganizational Cooperation: Toward a Research Agenda," *Academy of Management Journal* 39, no. 1 (February 1995): 7–23.

19. See Relational Coordination Research Collaborative, Brandeis University, http://rcrc.brandeis.edu/; and Jody Hoffer Gittell, *High Performance Healthcare: Using the Power of Relationships to Achieve Quality, Efficiency, and Resilience* (New York: McGraw-Hill Education, 2009).

20. Jody Hoffer Gittell, *The Southwest Airlines Way* (New York: McGraw-Hill, 2003), 20.

21. We thank Jody for sharing this new article in development: Jody Hoffer Gittell and Caroline K. Logan, "Developing Relational Coordination: What We Are Learning" (2014), under preparation.

22. Jane E. Dutton, Jacoba M. Lilius, and Jason M. Kanov, "The Transformative Potential of Compassion at Work," in *Handbook of Transformative Cooperation: New Designs and Dynamics*, eds. Sandy K. Piderit, Ronald E. Fry, and David L. Cooperrider (Stanford, CA: Stanford University Press, 2007), 107–26.

23. Günter K. Stahl, Ingmar Björkman, Elaine Farndale, Shad S. Morris, Jaap Paauwe, Philip Stiles, Jonathan Trevor, and Patrick Wright, "Six Principles of Effective Global Talent Management," *Sloan Management Review* 53, no. 2 (December 21, 2011): 25–42.

24. Watch CEO Jeff Weiner's "Conversation on Compassion" at Stanford University: http://ccare.stanford.edu/videos/conversations-on-compassion-with-jeff-weiner/.

25. Jane E. Dutton and Lindsay Reed, "A Values-based Approach to Candidate Selection: LinkedIn Intern Interviews," Center for Positive Organizations (Ann Arbor, MI: WDI Publishing, December 3, 2014).

26. We wrote about this in our paper "The contours and consequences of compassion at work," referenced above.

27. Findings from Gallup's *State of the Global Workplace* report: http://www.gallup .com/services/178517/state-global-workplace.aspx.

28. Adam M. Grant, "Giving Time, Time After Time: Work Design and Sustained Employee Participation in Corporate Volunteering," *Academy of Management Review* 37, no. 4 (October 1, 2012): 589–615.

29. Gallup's research linking employee engagement and customer metrics: http:// www.gallup.com/businessjournal/187748/holiday-stress-managers-retail-workers.aspx?g_source=retail&g_medium=search&g_campaign=tiles.

30. Andre S. Abramchuk, Michael R. Manning, and Robert A. Carpino, "Compassion for a Change: A Review of Research and Theory," *Research in Organizational Change and Development* 21 (2013): 201–32.

31. Karen Golden-Biddle and Jina Mao, "What Makes an Organizational Change Process Positive?" in *The Oxford Handbook of Positive Organizational Scholarship*, eds. Kim S. Cameron and Gretchen M. Spreitzer (New York: Oxford University Press, 2012), 763.

32. Scott Sonenshein, "Treat Employees as Resources, Not Resisters," in Jane Dutton and Gretchen Spreitzer, *How to Be a Positive Leader* (San Francisco: Berrett-Koehler Publishers, 2014): 136–46.

33. Donde A. Plowman, Lakami T. Baker, Tammy E. Beck, Mukta Kulkarni, Stephanie Thomas Solansky, and Deandra V. Travis, "Radical Change Accidentally: The Emergence and Amplification of Small Change," *Academy of Management* 50, no. 3 (June 1, 2007): 515–43.

34. Gerald F. Davis, *The Vanishing American Corporation: Navigating the Hazards of a New Economy* (Oakland, CA: Berrett-Koehler Publishers, 2016).

35. Regina F. Bento, "When the Show Must Go On: Disenfranchised Grief in Organizations," *Journal of Managerial Psychology* 9, no. 6 (1994): 35–44.

PART TWO: Awakening Compassion in Our Work Lives

1. See http://blogs.helsinki.fi/copassion/in-english/.

CHAPTER 3: Noticing: The Portal to Awakening Compassion

1. Max H. Bazerman, *The Power of Noticing: What the Best Leaders See* (New York: Simon and Schuster, 2014), 181.

2. Edgar H. Schein, *Humble Inquiry: The Gentle Art of Asking Instead of Telling* (San Francisco: Berrett-Koehler Publishers, 2013).

3. Eric J. Cassell, "Diagnosing Suffering: A Perspective," *Annals of Internal Medicine* 131, no. 7 (October 5, 1999): 531–34.

4. Elaine Scarry, *The Body in Pain: The Making and Unmaking of the World* (New York: Oxford University Press, 1985).

CHAPTER 4: Interpreting: The Key to Responding with Compassion

1. Peter J. Frost, Jane E. Dutton, Monica C. Worline, and Annette Wilson, "Narratives of Compassion in Organizations," in *Understanding Emotion at Work*, ed. Stephen Fineman (London: SAGE Publications Ltd., 2003), 40.

2. Paul W. B. Atkins and Sharon K. Parker, "Understanding Individual Compassion in Organizations: The Role of Appraisals and Psychological Flexibility," *Academy of Management Review* 37, no. 4 (October 1, 2012): 524–46.

3. Daniel Kahneman, *Thinking, Fast and Slow* (New York: Farrar, Straus and Giroux, 2011).

4. Jennifer L. Goetz, Dacher Keltner, and Emiliana Simon-Thomas, "Compassion: An Evolutionary Analysis and Empirical Review," *Psychological Bulletin* 136, no. 3 (May 2010): 351–74.

5. Daniel Martin, Emma Seppälä, Yotam Heineberg, Tim Rossomando, James Doty, Philip Zimbardo, Ting-Ting Shiue, Rony Berger, and YanYan Zhou, "Multiple Facets of Compassion: The Impact of Social Dominance Orientation and Economic Systems Justification," *Journal of Business Ethics* 129, no. 1 (2015): 237–49.

6. Candace Clark, *Misery and Company: Sympathy in Everyday Life* (Chicago: University of Chicago Press, 1997).

7. See Sharon Salzberg, "Fierce Compassion," *Huffington Post*, August 14, 2012, http://www.huffingtonpost.com/sharon-salzberg/fierce-compassion_b_1775414.html. See also Sharon Salzberg, *Real Happiness at Work* (New York: Workman Publishing, 2014).

8. Kerry Patterson, Joseph Grenny, Ron McMillan, and Al Switzler, *Crucial Conversations: Tools for Talking When Stakes Are High* (New York: McGraw-Hill, 2002).

9. Quy N. Huy, "In praise of middle managers," *Harvard Business Review* 78, no. 8 (September 2001): 72–79, 160.

10. Lloyd E. Sandelands, "On Taking People Seriously: An Apology, to My Students Especially," *Journal of Business Ethics* 126, no. 4 (February 2015): 603–11.

11. Martin Buber, *I and Thou*, trans. Walter Kaufman (New York: Touchstone, 1970).

12. Thupten Jinpa, *A Fearless Heart: How the Courage to Be Compassionate Can Transform Our Lives* (New York: Hudson Street Press, 2015).

13. Kristen R. Monroe, *The Heart of Altruism: Perceptions of a Common Humanity* (Princeton, NJ: Princeton University Press, 1996): 197.

14. Ibid., 206.

15. Ibid., 201.

16. Compassion activists such as Ari Cowan at the International Center for Compassionate Organizations offer training in compassion-based conflict resolution. Compassion-focused therapy approaches described by scholars like Paul Gilbert and compassion coaching for leaders, such as that described by Richard Boyatzis, can also be resources.

17. Emma Seppälä, "Why Compassion Is a Better Managerial Tactic Than Toughness," *Harvard Business Review* (blog), May 7, 2015, https://hbr.org/2015/05/why-compassion-is-a-better-managerial-tactic-than-toughness.

18. Allison Rimm, "To Guide Difficult Conversations, Try Using Compassion," *Harvard Business Review* (blog), June 19, 2013, https://hbr.org/2013/06/to-guide-difficult-conversatio.

19. Ryan Fehr and Michele J. Felfand, "The Forgiving Organization: A Multilevel Model of Forgiveness at Work," *Academy of Management Review* 37, no. 4 (2012): 664–88.

20. Lonni Collins Pratt and Daniel Homan, *Radical Hospitality: Benedict's Way of Love* (Brewster, MA: Paraclete Press, 2002), 16.

CHAPTER 5: Feeling: The Bridge to Compassionate Action

1. Leslie Jamison, *The Empathy Exams* (Minneapolis: Graywolf Press, 2014).

2. Cendri A. Hutcherson, Emma M. Seppälä, and James J. Gross, "The neural correlates of social connection," *Cognitive, Affective, & Behavioral Neuroscience* 15, no. 1 (March 2015): 1–14.

3. Jean Decety and William Ickes, *The Social Neuroscience of Empathy* (Cambridge, MA: The MIT Press, 2011). For a readable summary of evidence on empathy: http://blogs.scientificamerican.com/moral-universe/empathy-as-a-choice/.

4. C. Daryl Cameron and B. Keith Payne, "Escaping Affect: How Motivated Emotion Regulation Creates Insensitivity to Mass Suffering," *Journal of Personality and Social Psychology* 100, no. 1 (2011): 1–15.

5. See Jamil Zaki, "Empathy as a choice 3: 'Growing' empathy," *Scientific American*, August 22, 2013, http://blogs.scientificamerican.com/moral-universe/empathy-as-a-choice-3-e2809cgrowinge2809d-empathy/.

6. C. Daniel Batson, "These Things Called Empathy: Eight Related but Distinct Phenomena," in *The Social Neuroscience of Empathy*, eds. Jean Decety and William Ickes (Cambridge, MA: The MIT Press, 2011), 3–16.

7. Dacher Keltner, *Born to Be Good* (New York: W. W. Norton & Company, 2009); Matthew D. Lieberman, *Social: Why Our Brains Are Wired to Connect* (New York: Crown Publishing Group, 2013).

8. Naomi I. Eisenberger, Matthew D. Lieberman, and Kipling D. Williams, "Does Rejection Hurt? An fMRI Study of Social Exclusion," *Science* 302 (October 10, 2003), http://www.scn.ucla.edu/pdf/Cyberball290.pdf.

9. For an accessible summary of this kind of research, see Mo, "Feeling the pain of others," *ScienceBlogs*, December 17, 2009, http://scienceblogs.com/neurophilosophy/2009/12/17/feeling-the-pain-of-others/.

10. Sara D. Hodges and Kristi J. K. Klein, "Regulating the costs of empathy: The price of being human," *Journal of Socio-Economics* 30 (2001): 437–52.

11. For an overview, see C. Daryl Cameron, "Can You Run Out of Empathy?" *Greater Good*, University of California, Berkeley, May 20, 2013, http://greater-good.berkeley.edu/article/item/run_out_of_empathy.

12. William A. Kahn, "To Be Fully There: Psychological Presence at Work," *Human Relations* 45, no. 4 (April 1992): 321–49.

13. John Shotter, "The Manager as Practical Author: A Rhetorical-Responsive, Social Constructionist Approach to Social Organizational Problems," in *Management and Organizations: Relationship Alternatives to Individualism*, eds. Dian Marie Hosking, H. Peter Dachler, and Kenneth J. Gergen (Aldershot, UK: Avebury, 1995), 127.

14. Karla McLaren, *The Art of Empathy: A Complete Guide to Life's Most Essential Skill* (Boulder, CO: Sounds True, 2013).

15. Joan Halifax, "G.R.A.C.E. for Nurses: Cultivating Compassion in Nurse/Patient Interactions," *Journal of Nursing Education and Practice* 4, no. 1 (2014): 126.

16. Patricia Benner, Christine A. Tanner, and Catherine A. Chesla, *Expertise in Nursing Practice: Caring, Clinical Judgment, and Ethics* (New York: Spring Publishing Company, 1996).

17. Laura E. M. Leong, Annmarie Cano, Lee H. Wurm, Mark A. Lumley, and Angelia M. Corley, "A Perspective-Taking Manipulation Leads to Greater Empathy and Less Pain During the Cold Pressor Task," *Journal of Pain* 16, no. 11 (November 2015): 1176–85; Deborah Way and Sarah J. Tracy, "Conceptualizing Compassion as Recognizing, Relating and (Re)acting: A Qualitative Study of Compassionate Communication at Hospice," *Communication Monographs* 79, no. 3 (2012), 292–315.

18. Ellen J. Langer, *Mindfulness* (Boston: Addison-Wesley Publishing Company, 1989).

19. Shian-Ling Keng, Moria J. Smoski, and Clive J. Robins, "Effects of Mindfulness on Psychological Health: A Review of Empirical Studies," *Clinical Psychology Review* 31, no. 6 (August 31, 2011): 1041–56.

20. Frans de Waal, *The Age of Empathy: Nature's Lessons for a Kinder Society* (New York: Harmony Books, 2009), 213.

21. Piercarlo Valdesolo and David DeSteno, "Synchrony and the Social Tuning of Compassion," *Emotion* 11, no. 2 (April 2011): 262–66.

22. Frank Martela, "Caring Connections—Compassionate mutuality in the organizational life of a nursing home." PhD diss., Aalto University, 2012, http://urn.fi/URN:ISBN:978-952-60-4848-2.

23. We quoted from Ralph's story in our chapter of Stephen Fineman, *Understanding Emotion at Work* (London: SAGE Publications Ltd., 2003), 40.

24. Edward M. Hallowell, "The Human Moment at Work," *Harvard Business Review* 77, no. 1 (January–February 1999): 60.

CHAPTER 6: Acting: The Moves That Alleviate Suffering at Work

1. Margaret Vickers, "Taking a compassionate turn for workers with multiple sclerosis (MS): Towards the facilitation of management learning," *Management Learning* 42, no. 1 (February 2011): 49–65.

2. Manfred F. R. Kets de Vries and Katharina Balazs, "The Downside of Downsizing," *Human Relations* 50, no. 1 (January 1997): 11–50.

3. Mika Kivimäki, Jussi Vahtera, Jaana Pentti, and Jane E. Ferrie, "Factors underlying the effect of organisational downsizing on health of employees: Longitudinal cohort study," *British Medical Journal* 320, no. 7240 (April 2000): 971–75, http://www.ncbi.nlm.nih.gov/pmc/articles/PMC27336/.

4. Joshua D. Margolis and Andrew Molinsky, "Navigating the Bind of Necessary Evils: Psychological Engagement and the Production of Interpersonally Sensitive Behavior," *Academy of Management Journal* 51, no. 5 (October 1, 2008): 847–72.

5. Jennifer K. Robbennolt, "Apologies and Medical Error," *Clinical Orthopaedics and Related Research* 467, no. 2 (February 2009): 376–82.

6. Peter Frost and Sandra Robinson, "The Toxic Handler: Organizational Hero-and Casualty," *Harvard Business Review* 77, no. 4 (July–August 1999): 96–106, 185.

7. Paul Gilbert, *The Compassionate Mind: A New Approach to Life's Challenges* (Oakland, CA: New Harbinger Publications, 2009).

8. Brené Brown, *The Power of Vulnerability: Teachings on Authenticity, Connection, and Courage*, read by author (Louisville, CO: Sounds True Audio, 2012).

PART THREE: Awakening Compassion Competence in Organizations

CHAPTER 7: Envisioning Compassion Competence

1. Jane E. Dutton, Peter J. Frost, Monica C. Worline, Jacoba M. Lilius, and Jason M. Kanov, "Leading in Times of Trauma," *Harvard Business Review* 80, no. 1 (January 2002): 54–61, 125.

2. Jerry Sternin and Robert Choo, "The Power of Positive Deviancy," *Harvard Business Review* 78, no. 1 (January–February 2000): 14–15.

3. Edward H. Powley, "The Process and Mechanisms of Organizational Healing," *Journal of Applied Behavioral Science* 49, no. 1 (March 2013): 42–68.

4. Dean A. Shepherd and Trenton A. Williams, "Local venturing as compassion organizing in the aftermath of a natural disaster: The role of localness and community in reducing suffering," *Journal of Management Studies* 51, no. 6 (September 2014): 952–94.

5. Martha S. Feldman, "Resources in emerging structures and processes of change," *Organization Science* 15, no. 3 (2004): 295–309.

6. Martha Feldman and Monica Worline, "The Practicality of Practice Theory," *Academy of Management Learning & Education* 15, no. 2 (June 1, 2016): 304–24.

CHAPTER 8: Understanding Compassion Competence

1. Jane E. Dutton, Monica C. Worline, Peter J. Frost, and Jacoba Lilius, "Explaining Compassion Organizing," *Administrative Science Quarterly* 51, no. 1 (March 2006): 59–96.

2. W. Richard Scott and Gerald F. Davis, "Networks In and Around Organizations," in *Organizations and Organizing: Rational, Natural, and Open System Perspectives* (New York: Pearson Prentice Hall, 2007), 278.

3. David Easley and Jon Kleinberg, *Networks, Crowds, and Markets: Reasoning About a Highly Connected World* (Cambridge, UK: Cambridge University Press, 2010), 1–20.

4. Rob Cross, Wayne Baker, and Andrew Parker, "What Creates Energy in Organizations," *MIT Sloan Management Review*, last modified July 15, 2003, http://sloanreview.mit.edu/article/what-creates-energy-in-organizations/.

5. Jane E. Dutton and Emily D. Heaphy, "The Power of High Quality Connections," in *Positive Organizational Scholarship*, eds. Kim S. Cameron, Jane E. Dutton, and Robert E. Quinn (San Francisco: Berrett-Koehler Publishers, 2003), 263–78.

6. Jane E. Dutton, *Energize Your Workplace: How to Create and Sustain High-Quality Connections at Work* (San Francisco: Jossey-Bass, 2003).

7. Edgar H. Schein, *Organizational Culture and Leadership*, 4th ed. (San Francisco: Jossey-Bass, 2010).

8. Lynn P. Wooten and Patricia Crane, "Generating Dynamic Capabilities through a Humanistic Work Ideology," *American Behavioral Scientist* 47, no. 6 (February 2004): 848–66.

9. Sigal G. Barsade and Olivia A. O'Neill, "What's Love Got to Do with It? A Longitudinal Study of the Culture of Companionate Love and Employee and Client Outcomes in a Long-term Care Setting," *Administrative Science Quarterly* 59, no. 4 (December 2014): 551–98.

10. Jennifer Crocker and Amy Canevello, "Consequences of Self-Image and Compassionate Goals," *Advances in Experimental Social Psychology* 45 (2012): 229–77.

11. Daniel Katz and Robert L. Kahn, *The Social Psychology of Organizations* (New York: John Wiley & Sons, 1978).

12. Amy Wrzesniewski and Jane E. Dutton, "Crafting a job: Revisioning employees as active crafters of their work," *Academy of Management Review* 26, no. 2 (2001): 179–201.

13. Ronald J. Iannotti, "Effect of role-taking experiences on role taking, empathy, altruism, and aggression," *Developmental Psychology* 14, no. 2 (March 1978): 119–24.

14. Amy Wrzesniewski, Jane E. Dutton, and Gelaye Debebe, "Interpersonal Sensemaking and the Meaning of Work," *Research in Organizational Behavior* 25 (December 2002): 93–135.

15. Laura Madden, Dennis Duchon, Timothy Madden, and Donde Plowman, "Emergent organizational capacity for compassion," *Academy of Management Review* 37, no. 4 (October 1, 2012): 689–708.

16. Martha S. Feldman and Brian T. Pentland, "Reconceptualizing Organizational Routines as a Source of Flexibility and Change," *Administrative Science Quarterly* 48 (March 2003): 94–118.

17. Barbara L. Fredrickson, *Love 2.0: How Our Supreme Emotion Affects Everything We Feel, Think, Do, and Become* (New York: Hudson Street Press, 2013).

18. Davide Nicolini, *Practice Theory, Work, and Organization* (Oxford, UK: Oxford University Press, 2012).

19. Peter L. Berger and Thomas Luckmann, *The Social Construction of Reality: A Treatise in the Sociology of Knowledge* (New York: Anchor Books, 1966).

20. Practitioners, see Stephen Denning, *The Leader's Guide to Storytelling* (New York: Jossey-Bass, 2011). Academics, see Barbara Czarniawska, *Narrating the Organization: Dramas of Institutional Identity* (Chicago: The University of Chicago Press, 1997).

21. We wrote about this in our paper "The contours and consequences of compassion at work," referenced above.

22. Thomas B. Lawrence and Sally Maitlis, "Care and Possibility: Enacting an Ethic of Care Through Narrative Practice," *Academy of Management Review* 37, no. 4 (October 1, 2012): 641–63.

23. Barbara Czarniawska-Joerges and Rolf Wolff, "Leaders, Managers, Entrepreneurs on and off the Organizational Stage," *Organization Studies* 12, no. 4 (October 1991): 529–46.

24. Robert E. Quinn, *The Positive Organization: Breaking Free from Conventional Cultures, Constraints, and Beliefs* (Oakland, CA: Berrett-Koehler Publishers, 2015).

CHAPTER 9: Designing for Compassion Competence

1. Gretchen M. Spreitzer and Scott Sonenshein, "Positive Deviance and Extraordinary Organizing," *Positive Organizational Scholarship* (2003): 207–24.

2. Jacoba M. Lilius, Monica C. Worline, Jane E. Dutton, Jason M. Kanov, and Sally Maitlis, "Understanding compassion capability," *Human Relations* 64, no. 7 (July 2011): 873–99.

3. Emily Stoper, "Women's Work, Women's Movement: Taking Stock," *Annals of the American Academy of Political and Social Science* 515 (May 1991): 151–62, http://www.jstor.org/stable/1046935.

4. These are conditions that foster high-quality connections as articulated in Jane's book *Energize Your Workplace*, referenced earlier.

5. Laura E. McClelland and Timothy J. Vogus, "Compassion Practices and HCAHPS: Does Rewarding and Supporting Workplace Compassion Influence Patient Perceptions?" *Health Services Research* 49, no. 5 (October 2014): 1670–83.

6. Candace Clark, *Misery and Company: Sympathy in Everyday Life* (Chicago: University of Chicago Press, 1997).

7. Dale T. Miller and Deborah A. Prentice, "Psychological Levers of Behavioral Change," in *The Behavioral Foundations of Public Policy*, ed. Eldar Shafir (Princeton, NJ: Princeton University Press, 2012), 301–309. See also Zaki, "Empathy as a choice 3," http://blogs.scientificamerican.com/moral-universe/empathy-as-a-choice-3-e2809cgrowinge2809d-empathy/.

8. Monica C. Worline and Sarah Boik, "Leadership lessons from Sarah: Values-based leadership as everyday practice," in *Leading with Values: Positivity, Virtue, and High Performance*, eds. Kim Cameron and Edward Hess (Cambridge, UK: Cambridge University Press, 2006): 108–31.

9. This story is adapted from Amy Edmondson, *Teaming to Innovate* (San Francisco: Jossey-Bass, 2013).

10. Ibid., 42.

11. Ibid.

12. Ace V. Simpson, "Normal Compassion: A framework for compassionate decision making," *Journal of Business Ethics* 119, no. 4 (January 2014): 473–91.

13. Warren Nilsson and Tana Paddock, "Social Innovation From the Inside Out," *Stanford Social Innovation Review* (Winter 2014), http://ssir.org/articles/entry/social_innovation_from_the_inside_out.

14. See Lloyd E. Sandelands, *Feeling and Form in Social Life* (Lanham, MD: Rowman & Littlefield, 1997); and Johan Huizinga, *Homo Ludens: A Study of the Play-element in Culture* (Boston: The Beacon Press, 1955).

15. Seung-Yoon Rhee, Jane E. Dutton, Richard P. Bagozzi, "Making Sense of Organizational Actions in Response to Tragedy: Virtue Frames, Organizational Identification and Organizational Attachment," *Journal of Management, Spirituality & Religion* 3, no. 1–2 (2006): 34–59.

16. Jonathan Haidt, "The Moral Emotions," in *Handbook of Affective Sciences*, eds. Richard J. Davidson, Klaus R. Scherer, and H. Hill Goldsmith (Oxford, UK: Oxford University Press, 2003), 852–70.

CHAPTER 10: Leading for Compassion Competence

1. Ronald A. Heifetz, *Leadership Without Easy Answers* (Boston: Harvard University Press, 1994), 69.

2. Dutton et al., "Leading in Times of Trauma": 54–61. See also Monica C. Worline and Jane E. Dutton, "How Leaders Shape Compassion Processes in Organizations," *Oxford Handbook of Compassion Science* (forthcoming, Oxford University Press).

3. James M. Burns, *Leadership* (New York: Harper & Row, 1978); Bernard M. Bass, *Leadership and Performance Beyond Expectations* (New York: Free Press, 1985).

4. Richard Boyatzis and Annie McKee, *Resonant Leadership: Renewing Yourself and Connecting with Others Through Mindfulness, Hope, and Compassion* (Boston: Harvard Business School Press, 2005).

5. Katie Smith Milway and Alex Goldmark, "Four Ways to Cultivate a Culture of Curiosity," *Creativity* (blog), *Harvard Business Review*, September 18, 2013, https://hbr.org/2013/09/four-ways-to-cultivate-a-culture-of-curiosity.

6. Boyatzis and McKee, *Resonant Leadership*.

7. Susan T. Fiske, "Controlling Other People: The Impact of Power on Stereotyping," *American Psychologist* 48 (2013): 621–28.

8. Dacher Keltner, *The Power Paradox* (New York: Penguin, 2016).

9. Simon Sinek, foreword to *Everybody Matters*, by Bob Chapman and Raj Sisodia (New York: Penguin Random House, 2015), xi.

10. *Everybody Matters*, 67.

11. Ibid., 68.

12. Ibid., 90.

13. Ibid., 91.

14. Jeff Weiner, "Managing Compassionately," *LinkedIn Pulse*, October 15, 2012, https://www.linkedin.com/pulse/20121015034012-22330283-managing-compassionately.

15. John Mackey and Rajendra Sisodia, *Conscious Capitalism: Liberating the Heroic Spirit of Business* (Boston: Harvard Business Review Press, 2013), 181.

16. You can read more about this program in James R. Bradley, "Bridging the Cultures of Business and Poverty: Welfare to Career at Cascade Engineering," *Stanford Social Innovation Review*, Spring 2003, http://ssir.org/articles/entry/bridging_the_cultures_of_business_and_poverty.

17. Peter J. Frost, Jane E. Dutton, Sally Maitlis, Jacoba M. Lilius, Jason M. Kanov, and Monica C. Worline, "Seeing Organizations Differently: Three Lenses on Compassion," in *The SAGE Handbook of Organization Studies*, 2nd ed., eds. Stewart Clegg, Cynthia Hardy, Thomas B. Lawrence, and Walter R. Nord (London: SAGE Publications, 2006), 843–66.

18. This account of events at Reuters is taken from Jane E. Dutton, Ryan Quinn, and Robert Pasick, *The Heart of Reuters* (Ann Arbor, MI: University of Michigan: Center for Positive Organizational Scholarship, 2002).

19. Ibid., 5.

20. Ibid., 7.

21. Ibid.

22. Ibid., 9.

23. Ibid., 8.

PART FOUR: Blueprints for Awakening Compassion at Work

1. Jason Kanov, Edward Powley, and Neil Walshe, "Is it OK to care? How compassion falters and is courageously accomplished in the midst of uncertainty," *Human Relations* (forthcoming 2016).

CHAPTER 13: Overcoming Obstacles to Compassion at Work

1. Matthieu Ricard, *Altruism: The Power of Compassion to Change Yourself and the World* (New York: Little, Brown and Company, 2013).

2. Ace V. Simpson, Stewart R. Clegg, Miguel P. Lopes, Miguel Pina e Cunha, Arménio Rego, and Tyrone Pitsis, "Doing Compassion or Doing Discipline? Power Relations and the Magdalene Laundries," *Journal of Political Power* 7, no. 2 (June 16, 2014): 253–74, doi: 10.1080.

3. Arne Carlsen, Stewart Clegg, and Reidar Gjersvik, *Idea Work* (Norway: J W Cappelens Forlag AS, 2012).

4. Christine Pearson and Christine Porath, *The Cost of Bad Behavior: How Incivility Is Damaging Your Business and What to Do About It* (New York: Portfolio Hardcover, 2009).

5. Martha C. Nussbaum, *Upheavals of Thought: The Intelligence of Emotions* (Cambridge, UK: Cambridge University Press, 2003), 343.

6. Bethany McLean and Peter Elkind, *The Smartest Guys in the Room: The Amazing Rise and Scandalous Fall of Enron* (New York: Penguin Group, 2003).

7. Andrew L. Molinsky, Adam M. Grant, and Joshua D. Margolis, "The Bedside Manner of Homo Economicus: How and Why Priming an Economic Schema Reduces Compassion," *Organizational Behavior and Human Decision Processes* 119, no. 1 (2012): 27–37.

8. Charles Figley, ed. *Compassion Fatigue: Coping with Secondary Traumatic Stress Disorder in Those Who Treat the Traumatized* (New York: Brunner-Routledge, 1995).

9. Sherry Turkle, *Alone Together: Why We Expect More from Technology and Less from Each Other* (New York: Basic Books, 2011), 165.

10. Mary Ann Hazen, "Societal and workplace responses to perinatal loss: Disenfranchised grief or healing connection," *Human Relations* 56, no. 2 (2003): 147–66.

11. Nussbaum, *Upheavals of Thought*, 343.

12. Pratt and Homan, *Radical Hospitality*, 115.

13. Gail Whiteman, "Management Studies That Break Your Heart," *Journal of Management Inquiry* 19, no. 4 (December 2010): 328–37.

14. Pratt and Homan, *Radical Hospitality*, 197–200.

EPILOGUE

1. Pema Chödrön, *When Things Fall Apart* (Boston: Shambhala Publications, 1997): 121.

2. Emma Seppälä, *The Happiness Track: How to Apply the Science of Happiness to Accelerate Your Success* (New York: HarperCollins, 2016).

3. Alice Calaprice, *The New Quotable Einstein* (Princeton, NJ: Princeton University Press, 2005), 206.

4. Robert Wuthnow, *Acts of Compassion: Caring for Others and Helping Ourselves* (Princeton, NJ: Princeton University Press, 1991), 309.

5. Nancy S. Alder and André L. Delbecq, "Twenty-first Century Leadership: A Return to Beauty," *Journal for Business Ethics* (forthcoming 2016), 18.

6. Lloyd E. Sandelands, *Being at Work* (Lanham, MD: University Press of America, 2014).

7. Peter Senge, C. Otto Scharmer, Joseph Jaworski, and Betty Sue Flowers, *Presence: An Exploration of Profound Change in People, Organizations, and Society* (New York: Doubleday, 2005.

8. Quoted in an interview: Xavier Le Pinchon, "The Fragility at the Heart of Humanity," *On Being with Krista Tippett*, July 29, 2016, http://www.onbeing.org/program/xavier-le-pichon-the-fragility-at-the-heart-of-humanity/101.

9. James R. Doty, *Into the Magic Shop: A Neurosurgeon's Quest to Discover the Mysteries of the Brain and the Secrets of the Heart* (New York: Penguin Random House, 2016). There are also many compassion resources on the website of the center he founded: http://ccare.stanford.edu.

ACKNOWLEDGMENTS

MANY HANDS AND HEARTS CONTRIBUTED to bring this work to fruition. For everyone who participated in our research over the past twenty years, named here or not, a deep bow of thanks. Opening your organizations to us was like opening a window of light.

We owe a magnificent debt of gratitude to the members of the CompassionLab, who have been our constant companions on this journey. CompassionLab began with Peter Frost and Sally Maitlis at one end of a webcam that connected Vancouver with Ann Arbor, while Jane Dutton, Monica Worline, Jason Kanov, and Jacoba Lilius huddled around a computer monitor at the other end. Those were fun days of awakening to the wonder of studying and practicing compassion at work.

CompassionLab has since grown to include many researchers. Thank you to the CoPassion team in Helsinki, and to Ruth Blatt, Oana Branzei, Lindsay Cameron, Ashley Hardin, Suntae Kim, Sarah Konrath, Reut Livne-Tarandach, Laura Madden, Laura McClelland, Mrudula Nujella, Mandy O'Neill, Veronica Rabelo, Ace Simpson, and Kristina Workman. We have touched on some of your work in this book, but your scholarship is far more expansive than the small mentions here. We are honored to be your colleagues.

Many in our field whose support and encouragement has kept us going over the years can't be named here, but that doesn't diminish our thanks for your contributions. In particular, we want to recognize Sara Rynes, Jean Bartunek, and Joshua Margolis for their scholarly leadership, and Anne Tsui for focusing the 2012 Academy of Management on the theme Dare to Care. Thank you also to luminaries such as Robert Wuthnow, Martha Nussbaum, and Nel

Noddings for developing foundational ideas without which we could not proceed. We are grateful for the light that public figures like Oprah Winfrey, Arianna Huffington, and Krista Tippett shine on the topic of compassion, and are continually renewed and inspired by writer activists like Karen Armstrong and her Charter for Compassion, which has galvanized compassion architects worldwide. We are additionally grateful for the colleagueship of James Doty and Emma Seppälä at Stanford's Center for Compassion and Altruism Research and Education, which provides a treasured home for the science of compassion. And to our friends and colleagues in the Ross School of Business at the University of Michigan, and the faculty, staff, students, and resident executives at the Center for Positive Organizations, we extend a thousand thanks—you are generous and nurturing colleagues. Special thanks to Chris Murchison, a visiting leader at CPO, for showing us how to be a compassion architect—you inspire us.

We would not have been able to do this work without the support of Jane's husband and Monica's mentor, Lloyd (Lance) Sandelands. Lance's work has challenged us to raise our game for many years now. He is a tireless champion and an appreciative reader. He's also a wonderful chef and host, and our many dinner conversations are evidenced in every chapter. Our deepest thanks aren't enough.

The book also would not have come to be without the love of families and friends. True to her name, Clare was a source of light and handled everything with more grace than we can describe. Raleigh was a continuous source of joy, and Cara, Karl, and Emily have been our teachers along the way. Thanks for including Monica as an honorary member of the clan! Monica's work family pitched in with editing, research support, and patience while she wasn't available. A thousand petals of appreciation to Dennis, who was our first and deepest reader. To Bob, Tricia, Stephanie, and Jean, overflowing gratitude to have you as coworkers, along with Wendy, Dong, and Jessica. To Sarah Powell, double petals of appreciation for helping us to master the endnotes.

Finally, to Neal Maillet and the Berrett-Koehler family, we are honored that you believed in this idea, even when the going got tough. And to Sheryl Fullerton, who provided encouragement at critical times, as well as thoughtful and careful editing, we're so grateful to have you on our team. Thank you.

INDEX

ABOUT THE AUTHORS

© John Hall Portraits

Monica C. Worline, PhD, (left) is founder and CEO of EnlivenWork, an innovation organization that teaches businesses and others how to tap into courageous thinking, compassionate leadership, and the curiosity to bring their best work to life. She is a research scientist at Stanford University's Center for Compassion and Altruism Research and Education, and executive director of CompassionLab, the world's leading research collaboratory focused on compassion at work. Monica holds a lectureship at the Ross School of Business, University of Michigan, and is affiliate faculty at the Center for Positive Organizations.

Jane E. Dutton, PhD, (right) is the Robert L. Kahn Distinguished University Professor of Business Administration and Psychology at the Ross School of Business. She is a cofounder of the Center for Positive Organizations and passionate about cultivating human flourishing at work. Her research focuses on compassion, job crafting, high-quality connections, and meaning making at work. She has written more than one hundred articles and published thirteen books (see http://webuser.bus.umich.edu/janedut/), including *How to Be a Positive Leader: Small Actions, Big Impact*. She is a founding member of CompassionLab—visit us and read more about our research at www. compassionlab.org.

Berrett–Koehler
Publishers

Connecting people and ideas
to create a world that works for all

Dear Reader,

Thank you for picking up this book and joining our worldwide community of Berrett-Koehler readers. We share ideas that bring positive change into people's lives, organizations, and society.

To welcome you, we'd like to offer you a free e-book. You can pick from among twelve of our bestselling books by entering the promotional code **BKP92E** here: http://www.bkconnection.com/welcome.

When you claim your free e-book, we'll also send you a copy of our e-newsletter, the *BK Communiqué*. Although you're free to unsubscribe, there are many benefits to sticking around. In every issue of our newsletter you'll find

- A free e-book
- Tips from famous authors
- Discounts on spotlight titles
- Hilarious insider publishing news
- A chance to win a prize for answering a riddle

Best of all, our readers tell us, "Your newsletter is the only one I actually read." So claim your gift today, and please stay in touch!

Sincerely,

Charlotte Ashlock
Steward of the BK Website

Questions? Comments? Contact me at bkcommunity@bkpub.com.

MIX
Paper from
responsible sources
FSC® C016245
FSC
www.fsc.org

Certified
B
Corporation
bcorporation.net